Royalty, Religion, Sex

and Mystery

UNRAVELLING BIBLICAL TEXTS

AND

LONG STANDING QUESTIONS

A PROJECT OF THE FEDERATION OF JEWISH MEN'S CLUBS

RABBI CHARLES SIMON

FOREWARD BY RABBI DAVID WOLPE

TABLE OF CONTENTS

Section 3

FOREWARD

The rabbis of ancient times wrote midrashim—interpretations and inventions that filled in the gaps of the Bible, and helped us understand the meaning and motivations behind the stories. In order to write a modern midrash you need both learning and sensitivity to the text. You have to love the characters and inhabit their worlds.

Rabbi Chuck Simon's book is a book of modern interpretation and midrash. It takes the stories of the Bible, explains them and then helps them come to life. What did the Levite feel as a survivor when the ark fell and Uzzah was killed? What is the story of David confronting a giant supposed to teach later generations? Finally, how did the rabbis succeed in making their reading of the text the one that became Judaism as we know it?

Rabbi Simon is an ideal guide. Both a careful student of Jewish texts and a community leader, he knows the questions we ask, and the questions we need to ask. This book takes us through the twists of the tales with understanding, insight and a gentle hand. Prepare to enter an ancient age, but one that speaks to the world outside our windows. Walk with Rabbi Simon as he teaches us timeless lessons through some of history's most fascinating stories. Kings and commoners, royalty and rabbis, intimacy and mystery—the whole pageant of human life unfolds in the pages of this publication.

RABBI DAVID WOLPE
Sinai Temple
Los Angeles, Calif.
April, 2016

SEEKING HOLINESS AND SPIRITUALITY IN THE BIBLE

We grow up being taught that the Bible is holy. But even accepting that, its holiness isn't what stumps us. It's that when we read the Bible, we also seek to be spiritually stimulated, and that elusive quality sometimes leaves us feeling empty, or at best confused. Today most moderns are aware of the dangers of believing in the literal, most basic meaning of the text and as they look around, both within the Jewish world and without, they are conscious of the dangers of fundamentalism. Fortunately, as Jews we have the tools to look deeper for meaning, while retaining the holiness of the text as it is written. Initially, we may not be spiritually moved by what we read, but understanding our holy texts on a deeper, less literal level may open the door to finding that elusive spiritual quality we seek.

Some of us have heard our rabbis mention that the rabbis of old, those who lived at the beginning of the period of the Talmud, understood that in order to find meaning in the words of the Torah one needed to understand that it functioned on many levels. There is the simple plain meaning of the text (we call this the p'shat) and the meaning which is developed from the text, (we call this the drash, or the expository method). There is the hidden meaning of the text (we call this remez) and finally the secret meaning of the text (we call this the sod).[1] With these concepts in mind, scholars and mystics, who took the holiness of the Bible on faith, devoted their lives to seeking out the inner meanings contained within this work that they took to be divinely gifted.

A little more than a century ago, modern scholars, those who had acquired Western academic skills and backgrounds, began to explain the texts as divinely inspired. In other words, the study of the text trumps fundamentalist faith. This view recognizes that the Bible was written by people and not by a God who dictated it to Moses. At the same time, because they also believed in the holiness of the text, they explained that the conflicting views and complicated structure of the Bible was an opportunity to receive inspiration. Inspiration? How?

Among the many things we should thank the Talmudic rabbis for was their dividing the Bible into three levels of holiness.

---

[1] These four methods are known for their acronyms, PRDS, or Pardes.

The first level is the five books of Moses. This, the Torah, is our most holy book because it records the times when we allegedly heard God's voice or God acted through history. The second level of holiness is what we call Nevi'im, the Prophets including the early kings. These twenty one books begin with Joshua, include all the books of the Prophets, and conclude with the destruction of the First Temple. The final level, the least holy of the three, is referred to as Ketuvim, The Writings and is composed of the books of Psalms, Proverbs, Job, the five scrolls (megillot), Daniel, Ezra Nehemiah and the two books of Chronicles.

One can perhaps visualize a pyramid, with the first level of holiness being the theological foundations and the second and third levels as the top part being religious history.

But the basic question remains how do I, how can I be spiritually stimulated by these texts if I don't take them at face value?

This is the question I attempt to answer, at least for myself, by writing this book.

For more than a decade now, I have been studying the latest Bible research and have learned more about first and Second Temple history than I ever could have imagined. I incorporated that information into my understanding of certain trends and perhaps even core values embedded in the Bible. This prompted me to begin to teach Bible stories to adults, the stories they don't teach in Hebrew school, and five years ago I began to craft these new midrashim based on my what I learned in my reading and teaching.

Given what historians and archeologists have been learning about the historical periods during which the texts of the entire Bible took place, it becomes easier to view the men and women whose lives or certain aspects of their lives are recorded in the text, as real people addressing real situations. When we read it this way, the way we understand the text changes. It becomes more readable, more interesting and more appealing. This method hopefully strengthens our connection to the text and in doing so strengthens our religious identity. It might not make us want to pray, but it might encourage us to become more engaged. There is a bridge from the stories to the holiness and we are able to cross over it to reach the essence of what it means to be a Jew.

This book is composed of a series of essays and an occasional midrash each designed to shed light on questions that many of us have long wished to have answered. For example:

What's the difference between a Cohen and a Levite? Why are there Levites and what happened to them after the book of Deuteronomy?

What happened to the Ark and the Urim and Thumim?

What type of people were our kings?

Given that our kings of old were less great than we were taught as children, what can we learn from them?

What does it mean to use the phrase "A Good Samaritan" and should we use it at all?

What happened to the last kings of Israel?

How did the rabbis emerge as our religious leaders?

With this book, I hope to introduce this fascinating historical period, filled with stories of Royalty, Religion, Sex, and Mystery, and thus begin to explain the development of Judaism and the importance of our holy texts.

CHARLES SIMON

HOW TO BEST USE THIS WORK

This collection of essays and stories introduces you, the reader, to some of the personalities in the Bible as real people who had to deal with real situations. Of course (since history was written by the winners), most of what occurred has been conveyed, or shall we say constructed, in a manner that projects a vision of the past to a people living in exile several hundred years later for specific reasons. Reasons which will become apparent as you read the essays and stories that follow.

Every essay or story is based upon what I consider to be the most current research available. A tremendous amount of material has lately been published by biblical scholars and archeologists. My job and pleasure was to read as much as I could in order to answer my questions and then to interpret the material that hopefully will engage you. I rarely will quote an author because this was not meant to be a scholarly work. That's for scholars.

My contribution to this work is the spin, the interpretation, the conjecture. The material in the third and final section of this work was specifically written to answer what I consider to be some of the more basic questions about Jewish history that usually remain unanswered.

To use this text most effectively, go slowly. Ten minutes at a time should do it.

My advice is when you finish an essay or story, take a moment and ask yourself, what was he trying to do? Why did he give me this information in the way that he did? Is there a hidden lesson in the story or was the story essay solely written to provide me with a perspective to better understand Jewish life? I will try to guide you at the end of each section.

It all begins with the story of the Ark of the Covenant.

Section 1

UNRAVELLING THE BASICS OF
JEWISH RELIGIOUS ROYALTY

THE ARK OF THE COVENANT

An Autobiography

MY BIRTH

I remember the exact moment when I came into being. It was shortly after Moses was told to "make Me a sanctuary that I may dwell within it" (Exodus 25:8). I was shaped into a chest designed to house the two tablets which contained the ten holy phrases. When they placed those tablets within me, it warmed me and I woke up. I was given a name; they called me HaAron, the Ark of the Covenant (Numbers 10:35).

My consciousness developed slowly. In the beginning I learned how to listen. It took a long time for me to realize that I was able to hear. Noise over time became words. Words, often repeated. The more I heard the more I began to realize that I was able to distinguish tone, cadence and emotions. When I concentrated, I learned I could glow and rumble and even, if I worked at it very hard, rock from side to side.

I came to realize that I was created to fulfill three basic functions:

- The Holy one communicated to Moses in my presence
- Sacrifices took place in front of me. I must say, as I grew older and more mature, the wonder of these sacrifices, the burning filtered thankfully by incense, quickly faded
- Finally, and I think my most importantly and certainly my most far reaching function, was that the people of Israel experienced God's presence in front of me

When Moses concluded writing the Holy One's Teachings, he charged the Levites (who were entrusted with carrying me) to "Take this book of Teaching and place it inside the Ark of Covenant of the Lord your God, and let it remain there as a witness against you." (Deuteronomy 31:26)

That was my job. I was entrusted to carry the symbol of God's law as a testimony and a remembrance to the people. There were times when I could feel the people's faith and enthusiasm and when that occurred, the Tablets were as light as a feather. Later on, during the time of the Judges, it was like carrying a mountain.

When Joshua took over he arranged for me to be carried across the Jordan on the shoulders of the Levites (Deuteronomy 31:24 and Joshua 3:14-17). Hundreds of years later when they began to write my story, the storytellers imagined the Jordan River splitting the same way as the Red Sea had. Have you ever seen the Jordan? Trust me, even at its fullest, in springtime during a rainy season….storytellers, just like certain news stations, tend to exaggerate.

Joshua was a good leader. He respected me and I him. It was a good relationship. He did everything in his power to follow in the footsteps of Moses. Yes, the Levites carried me across the Jordan and yes they stood in the middle of the Jordan until all of the people had crossed. And maybe, just maybe, if the water hadn't separated it might have abutted some of their chests.

People were a lot shorter then than they are today.

They liked to carry me and I liked to be carried. During the siege of Jericho I was carried, well actually paraded around the city every day for seven days. It was grand. The priests preceded me, blowing all of their rams' horns. They dressed up and marched around the city, blowing and shouting and on the seventh day the walls just collapsed. It was quite a parade. I remember it so well because the Tablets were jostled around a lot and I almost lost them.

Joshua and his partner Caleb more or less governed everyone for the next forty or so years. If you remember, they were the two spies who saw the opportunity in the land and weren't afraid of the Canaanites. Caleb had just turned eighty-five and Joshua wasn't far behind. Both of them knew this couldn't last forever.

Joshua did the right thing. He empowered the priest Eliezer, Aaron's son, to establish a sanctuary at Gilgal. When Joshua died he was buried in the hill country of Ephraim and Gilgal became my home. Eliezer built an altar in Shiloh. Shiloh became my country house. Shiloh was five miles from Gilgal and five miles from Beth El. When Eliezer the son of Aaron died, he too was buried in hill country of Ephraim.

MY LIFE DURING THE TIME OF THE JUDGES

I'm not very good with time, but it must have been four or five generations after I settled in Shiloh and Gilgal before I learned to read. The priests used to leave documents in front of me when they were busy overseeing the construction of Solomon's Temple. I learned to read their financial records, which is what was placed in front of me. Never a book or good short story. Believe me I must have heard the phrase "Where are we going to find the money?" thousands of times.

During this period I was placed within the holy of holies, the innermost chamber of the Tabernacle.

I recently learned that writing, as we know it today, began to emerge in ancient Israel around the tenth century B.C.E. coinciding with the rise of the monarchy. At that time it was mostly royal correspondence and financial records, all of which were maintained by the emerging priestly class.

Fiction, well I call it fiction, wasn't going to come into being for another two or three hundred years. That's when my story, well my purported story, began to come together. By today's standards I would call the chronicle of my life a short story, "The Story of the Wanderings of the Ark of the Covenant". In time, it was integrated into the larger book, which came to be referred to simply as Judges.

But I wander. I'm told that often occurs with advanced age.

Shiloh was an important place. The book of Judges informs us (Judges 18:31) that the whole community of the Israelite people assembled at Shiloh, and set up the Tent of the meeting.

And, the heads of the ancestral house of the Levites approached the priest Eliezer, Joshua and the heads of the tribes and spoke to them at Shiloh in the land of Canaan asking for towns, since they couldn't own land. As a result they were integrated into the towns of the tribes and received pastureland.

We are also told that the annual feast of the Lord was held at Shiloh. (Judges 21:19)

Of course there was opposition. Phineas, another of Eliezer's sons, attempted to build an altar on the eastern shore of the Jordan but it didn't happen. After all there was only one of me and I was living in Shiloh, yes and on occasion I visited Gilgal and Shechem. Shechem was where the Covenant ceremony took place. (1 Samuel 3:21)

I really didn't want to leave Shiloh. Eliezer and his disciple Samuel took good care of me, but unfortunately Eliezer's two sons, Hophni and Phineas and the tribal elders had other ideas. You understand that the conquest of Canaan wasn't the slam dunk that is recorded in the book of Joshua. It was more of a gradual integration/migration highlighted by a number of territorial wars with different tribes. One of those tribes, the Philistines, was reluctant to give up their land. What a surprise! But Hophni and Phineas had serious aspirations and when the elders of Israel lost a battle, four thousand men had fallen and the Israelites were in danger of being overrun by the Philistines, the elders of the tribes looked to them to save the day. And they decided to take me into battle. They brought me with the cherubim that decorated my shoulders to their camp.

When the children of Israel saw me, they shouted with joy. It was so loud that the earth shook and the Philistines became frightened. "God has entered their camp", they cried. And the Philistines replied, "Woe unto us! Nothing like this has ever happened before. Who will save us from the power of the mighty God, the same God who struck the Egyptians with every type of plague in the wilderness"?

The Philistines reasoned that a loss could result in their enslavement just as the Hebrews had once been enslaved. They gathered their courage and went into battle and routed Israel! The Israelites fled to their home - thirty-thousand foot soldiers…lost.

Oh, and I was captured, and Eli's two sons were slain.

This came to be known as the battle of Aphek. (1 Samuel Chapter 4)

Can you imagine how I felt?

Being paraded in front of the enemy like I was a totem, a flag, a sign that the Israelites were favored by God! I was the place where God met man, not a standard, at least at that time, to be waived around.

Do you think they even considered how preposterous that was? I might have been the place where Israel came to speak to God but that wasn't an indication a surety that God would always be with them. If I was supposed to serve as a symbol of God's presence then it had to be warranted!

I was a prisoner of war.

The Philistines brought me to Ashdod. Ashdod was one of the five major Philistine cities and placed me inside the Temple of Dagon, well, actually they placed me next to him. And since I could move and shake and he couldn't do anything because he was a statue, the next morning the priests of Dagon entered the Temple and found him on the floor with broken arms and legs. Trust me, they were not happy. I have to admit, it felt pretty good.

Coincidentally, or not, the people suddenly became afflicted with a skin disease. In those days they called it hemorrhoids, but it was more like bubonic plague. (1 Samuel 6:4)

The people of Ashdod were not pleased. In fact they became worried and wanted to get rid of me, so they sent me to Gath. This didn't do much to improve brotherly love; I think it would be likened to the people of Manhattan sending the plague to Philadelphia.

Do you remember Gath? In just a few years, David would fight a giant named Goliath who came from Gath. Well, the plague travelled with me or with them and when it arrived in Gath, panic struck. They sent me to Ekron. The Ekronites weren't stupid and fearing the plague, consulted with their Philistine lords and decided I was too hot to handle and had to be returned to the Israelites. (1 Samuel 5:1-12)

This presented a problem. Who or how should a radioactive Ark be transported without causing more harm? The priests and diviners considered what to do with me for months. Finally they decided to return me with a bounty that reflected the good wishes from each of the five cities.

Okay, they decided what to do, but not how to get me there. Finally, and I mean finally and probably because they remembered what had happened in Egypt, they decided to "build a new cart, and attach it to two new cows that have-never been harnessed". Yes, pure virgin cows.

They placed me in the cart and filled it with lots of gold and send it off on its own, that is, without someone to lead the cows. And they decided to see what would occur.

They considered this to be a test. If the cows drew the cart toward Beth Shemesh they reasoned the Israelite God will have been pacified and their offer would have been accepted. On the other hand if the cows and the cart returned to Ekron, they knew that it was some other God who was enraged.

And that's exactly what they did, but…

When the people of Beth Shemesh who were reaping their wheat in the fields beheld me being drawn by the two rider-less cows, approach their land and stop. They looked at the cart and some of them opened my lid, looked inside and saw, UH OH! Well you know.

And then lots of things started to happen. The Levites picked me up and placed me on a large stone along with the gold objects. And God struck and killed the seventy men who had dared to open and look inside. It was a humiliating experience. When the five Philistine lords saw this they knew their offering had been accepted and they returned to Ekron.

Unfortunately, from the time I was captured and for the seven months when I was imprisoned, Shiloh had been destroyed.

I was orphaned.

Where was I supposed to live? The people of Beth Shemesh certainly didn't want me after The Big Guy got over-zealous and killed seventy of their finest. They consulted and consulted and decided that I belonged in Kiriath Yearim.

Kiariath Yearim was part of a network of cultic sites in the days leading up to David's move to Jerusalem It was in Judah and was already known as a sacred place. Like Shechem which was a major cultic site in the North. Kiariath Yearim, was the home of one of the branches of the Levite priesthood. In those days, different branches of the priesthood all worshipped Yahweh but they often considered different objects to be holy.

It was more or less a cousins' club. In the North, I was the object of reverence. In another city it could have been the Tent of Meeting, or the Urim and Thumim. It was even possible that many of our people's holy objects could have been housed in a central place and different peoples would understand them differently.

Life in Kiariath Yearim wasn't so bad. I was cared for by another branch of Aaron's line. That is until Saul became King.

MY LIFE DURING THE TIME OF THE KINGS

Saul was our first King. He was anointed by the prophet, priest and the last of the Judges, Samuel. (1 Samuel 11:15) It was a time when the Philistines and a number of other peoples were threatening. He gathered armies and fought battles on a series of fronts. But the most militant of all the peoples were the Philistines.

Saul brought me into battle at Gibeah. His son Jonathan had just won a skirmish and happened to be carrying the ephod. The ephod was one of the original priestly garments. It was something akin to a linen skirt that was adorned with jewels and was draped over the shoulders. It contained the Urim and Thumim. The Urim and Thumim was a vehicle of divination. Eventually it was lost or destroyed. It was probably a good thing; after all, how many decisions can a person make based on the role of the dice.

Saul's scouts observed the Philistines scattering in all directions and seized the moment brought me into the fray and won a major victory. It was a wise military decision, not a victory ordained by heaven.

David, his successor, was thirty years old when he was offered the crown of Judah. Seven years later in Hebron, the northern tribes asked him to be their king. It was the year 1000 B.C.E. (2 Samuel 5:1-5)

In order to unite the tribes under his rule, David sought to conquer Jerusalem and establish it as his city. It was at this point that he decided to bring me from the home of Abinadab in Baalim where I had been living since the Philistines set me free some twenty years ago, to Jerusalem. (Part of this story is detailed in the haftarah for parshat Shemini; but oh boy did the editors get this one wrong).

I had been living in the northern part of the country since Joshua had me carried across the Jordan River. I had fulfilled a major portion of the religious life of the people in the surrounding cities for nearly two hundred years. And then, all of a sudden, in an attempt to unite the northern and southern parts of Israel, David decided to have me brought to his new capital.

Imagine that! Imagine how the Levites and the people who lived in Shiloh, Beth El, and Shechem must have felt when their holiest object was commandeered and moved to Jerusalem.

Let's just say there were a few bumps in the road and David's grand plan took a little more time than he originally had imagined. Frankly, I didn't care where I was housed as long as there was shelter and I didn't get lonely. But the tribes in the North and the Levites who ministered to me cared a lot.

If you remember I was captured during the battle of Aphek. And for a number of reasons which I really don't want to discuss I ended up in Kiriath Yearim and lived there for twenty years. It was a good life. The people were extremely loyal, honest and attentive.

I lived in the home of Abinadab. Abinadab had three sons, Uzzah, Ahio and Eliezer. Yes, Eliezer could have been a descendant of Eliezer the son of Aaron, the Levite priest. They built me a special cart so I could travel in luxury.

I could have stayed there if it David hadn't had such visions of grandeur.

If my story is a novella, David's story is a novel.

Years, generations, centuries after his death the storytellers of the day, and believe me they were great storytellers, crafted a master story around the life of David. He was the shepherd who killed a giant and eventually became king. He was a person of lowly birth endowed with great nobility. A poet, a statesman and a warrior. The King whom the Lord loved the best and because of this promised to restore our people to the land which they had been given. I'm wandering again.

When David decided to have me relocated he "gathered all the chosen men of Israel, thirty thousand and of the hundreds with every leader and said to them, "let us bring the Ark of our God to us" (1 Chron 13: 1-13). And my faithful Uzzah travelled in the company of David accompanied by thirty thousand men as an escort on the road to Jerusalem.

It was a wonderful procession, I was carried in a newly built cart and Uzzah and his brother Ahio were my guides. They escorted me from their father's house with Uzzah walking on one side and Ahio in front. And David, David was at his best. He danced in front of me accompanied by harps, timbrels, sistrums and cymbals. But all of a sudden, when we reached the threshing floor of Nacshon, the oxen carrying me stumbled and the cart's balance shifted and I was about to fall, and Uzzah, oh my poor Uzzah reached out to prevent me from falling and breaking and shattering the tablets of the Covenant.

I don't think it was the oxen's fault, I think it could have been the northern priests who attempted to seize the moment and bring me back home. And Uzzah, poor Uzzah, Uzzah who had lived in my presence for twenty years, who had been assigned to drive me in a special cart constructed for the occasion. And who wanted to protect me from harm, which was his job as driver, gets killed for doing his job?

Do you actually think God would strike a man dead who sought to protect me? Who built my cart, sheltered me for years and walked alongside me to insure I didn't fall!

This little incident, this major incident, disrupted David's plans. The storytellers inform us that as a result of Uzzah's death, David became angry. Of course he was angry and not with Uzzah but with God. This was a major setback to the unification of Israel. It caused him to rethink bringing me to Jerusalem. And so I was deposited, in the house of Obed-edom the Gittite where I spent the next three months.

They were pleasant enough folk and as things quieted down I offered a little advice from time to time and Obed-edom and his family began to prosper. Success and prosperity often attracts wolves and when it was reported to David that the family was prospering, I was brought to Jerusalem. This time, no cart. We did it the old fashioned way on the shoulders of the Levites.

He certainly was smooth, that David. He brought me in joy and sacrificed in front of me and danced and distributed bread and cake to everyone. He wasn't taking any chances this time. He might have been the king of Judah and Israel, but without my presence in Jerusalem he couldn't secure the permanent allegiance of the northern tribes.

With me in Jerusalem the stage was set to build a Temple, but that's David's and his descendants' story, not mine.

My story is actually much simpler, no I take that back it is infinitely more complex. David's life was full of activity though during that time I became more of an object of veneration than the meeting place between man and God. Solomon built a magnificent Temple and placed me inside surrounded by a curtain and walls, and for the next four hundred odd years I was entombed. Lots of sacrifices, lots of incense, day after day after day, year after year after year … until the Babylonians conquered Jerusalem and took me with them as captured spoil.

MY LIFE AFTER THE EXILE FROM JERUSALEM

From that point on I became the lost Ark of God. There are those who claimed I was hidden, others who said, I was destroyed. When the Temple was rebuilt more than one hundred years later, I wasn't there. Ezra returned from Babylon with the Torah not with an Ark containing two tablets of stone.

Life became much more interesting in Babylonia than it ever was in Israel. City living had some serious advantages. People, lots of people with different ideas mingled with one another. We came to be called "Jews" and the Cohanim and Levites and others wrestled with being members of a small people in a larger more sophisticated society. And my consciousness expanded and I began to leak into the minds and hearts of an expanding maturing people. Scribes began to write our people's history on scrolls and recall that freedom and respect of one another were two of our core values.

Eventually, a few hundred years later, the people's beliefs matured and study began to parallel and eventually trump the sacrificial system. And they began to build houses, arks, in which to house the Torah. And they began to carrying it in a procession the way Joshua carried me at Jericho, around the sanctuary, in order to symbolize that God's presence resided in the study of Torah and that the study of Torah was a primary means of access to God.

And my spirit fused into these houses, these arks, and once again people would come and sit in my presence, well in the presence of You Know Who, and they would pray, or listen or look for solace and comfort and when that occurred tears would come to my metaphorical eyes because I knew I had finally come home.

THE LEVITES EMERGE

If you're interested in learning about the origins, importance and impact of the Levites, stop focusing on Jerusalem.

Everyone is focused on Jerusalem. The book of Joshua, Judges, and 1 Kings leads us to Jerusalem where David has transferred the ark. The book of 1 Kings records the history of and ultimate initial destruction of the Temple, which was in Jerusalem. Cyrus, the King of Persia and Media living in Babylon, permits Ezra to return to Jerusalem. Nearly five hundred years later, Jerusalem is conquered by the Romans as a result of the internecine fighting amidst rival political and religious groups in Jerusalem. And last, but perhaps not least, for centuries every morning and evening we turn east towards Jerusalem when we pray.

Clearly, Jewish history is Jerusalem-centric and closely connects us to a way of life that was guided by our priestly, usually Cohanic, tradition. The Cohanic tradition of presiding over sacrifices in the Temple existed until the Temple was destroyed in 70 C.E. Without a Temple the role of the priesthood in general, and specifically, that of the *Cohanim,* was unclear. Under the guidance of Rabbi Johanan ben Zachai, who lived through the period of the Temple's destruction and was the first person to be called rabbi, and his colleagues at Yavneh, legislation was passed which redirected and limited the Cohanic functions. Over time and in the absence of a Temple, the role of the priesthood devolved into what has become our present form, a form which acknowledges the priesthood mainly through the order in which people are called to the Torah.

Nowadays, even the limited roles and status conferred on *Cohanim* and *Levi'im* is changing. An increasing number of non-Orthodox congregatio- have replaced the hierarchical order of being called to the Torah with an egalitarian one and the few remaining customs allocated to the priesthood is becoming less and less visible. Today the *Cohanim* and *Levi'im* are priests without a well-defined role or a community to minister, although in some congregations outside Israel and most in Israel, the *Cohanim* pronounce the priestly blessing daily.

Cohanim and *Levi'im* are supposed to maintain some purity and not come in contact with the dead in hopes that at some future time they will be reinstated into a sacrificial cultic system which will take place in Jerusalem. They theoretically have to maintain their blood lines because in the event the Temple is rebuilt, they will rediscover their ancient calling, voluntarily relinquish their property, and allow themselves and their families to be supported by community offerings. Who would desire more than that?

(I can just imagine my late uncle Harry, the real estate mogul, who claimed to be a *Cohen,* continuing this claim after he was informed that his prop- erty would be forfeited.)

For more than two thousand years Judaism has allocated a higher status to the *Cohen,* and the reasons for their supremacy is more a result of the politics of Jewish history than the evidence found in the Torah.

What strikes me as odd is that I have been unable to find a reason, other than the link to a historical past and the hope for the building of a third Temple, for the legacy of the *Cohanim* to survive. Where and what was their spiritual message? Where and what were their moral teachings which ultimately became the values that shaped the Jewish people?

We could be looking in the wrong direction.

When we integrate into Jewish history that which also includes what we believe to have occurred outside of Jerusalem, we begin to understand how some of Judaism's most basic core values (study, learning and intellectual curiosity) developed and have become the foundation of Jewish culture. This view from outside Jerusalem also explains the history of the other priesthood, the Levites, and why they were important.

THE DEVELOPMENT OF THE TWO PRIESTHOODS

The biblical books of Numbers and Leviticus exclusively allocate the senior position of priesthood to the direct descendants of Aaron and a secondary status to the rest of the house of Levi from which they all descend. The superiority of Aaron's priestly line of the tribe of Levi is also stressed in the books of Exodus, Leviticus and Numbers where their tasks are clearly defined. According to Numbers, the Levites were supervised by Aaron's descendants. (Numbers 8:22)

The book of Deuteronomy describes the institution of priesthood differently. It considers the entire tribe of *Levi* to be priests who are called the sons of Levi, Levitical priests, or just priests. *(Cohanim)*. According to Deuteronomy, all Levites were fit to serve in the sanctuary, receive tithes, and had instructional responsibilities. The Deuteronomic view of the Levite differs from the other books.

We need to look beyond the Torah to periods of the Judges, Kings and First and Second Temples in order to understand how the institution of the Priesthood *(Cohen and Levi)* developed.

During the time of the Judges, the Levites were wanderers without permanent possessions and required tangible support from the wealthy along with other landless groups, like the widows, orphans and strangers in the gates. They travelled the length and breadth of the country and allegedly ministered to the people. It is feasible that some of them managed local shrines and offered sacrifices at different alters. Eli, the priest, who is mentioned in the story of the birth of Samuel as the one who managed the temple in Shiloh, is one example. (1 Samuel 1:9)

Prior to the Temple's construction a number of holy sites, such as Shiloh, Mitzpeh and Shechem existed. According to the book of Deuteronomy, these places of worship were outlawed during the reign of King Josiah, (622 B.C.E.) and replaced with the Jerusalem Temple's sacrificial system. The book of Deuteronomy, most of which was written during the Josianic period, mandates that all sacrifices/worship take place in Jerusalem. Jerusalem, for better or for worse, became the domain of the *Cohanim.*

Most scholars agree that the institutions of the priesthood, and specifically the High Priest, began to assume a central place in Jewish life at the time that Judaism developed as a national religion. This most likely occurred during the reigns of David and Solomon in the tenth century B.C.E.

Once the Temple had been constructed, the role of the Cohanim was to insure the continuation of the sacrificial system. This system, mandated by the Torah, was predicated on the fact that sacrifice was a regulated form of worship. The people offered sacrifices when they sinned or on mandated festivals, and the priests insured that the sacrifices were performed in the proper manner in order to please the Deity. That's why the Torah says that the sacrifices will be *pleasing fragrant offerings to God.* No one wants to mess with an angry God.

If the *Cohen* supervised the sacrificial system in Jerusalem, where were all the other descendants of Aaron many of whom had been ministering in the numerous holy places in ancient Israel? This is what I believe could be their story.

THE PRIESTHOOD FROM THE RISE OF THE MONARCHY THROUGH THE PERSIAN-GREEK PERIOD (Tenth Century B.C.E. - Third Century B.C.E.)

The Bible understands the priesthood to be a hereditary caste that served the people at shrines and in villages. There were probably several priestly families and, as social stratification increased, so did the conflict between them. Conventional scholarship acknowledges that King David had a priest named Zadok who ostensibly was the father of an extensive dynasty that controlled and centralized the priesthood up until Maccabean time. Specifically, this was from the times of the monarchy (around 1100 B.C.E.), through the exile (586), the return from Babylonia (539-445 B.C.E.), and up until the rise of the Maccabees (165 B.C.E.). The Hasmoneans, whom we refer to as the Maccabees, were another priestly (Aaronid) line that managed to replace the Zadokites.

Zadok's descendants, the Zadokites, gained and maintained their power because they were part of the governing class that served the monarchy. These same Zadokites were exiled when the Babylonians destroyed Jerusalem. Fifty odd years later, when Cyrus conquered Babylon, he called upon this priesthood to help him establish an empire in Yehud, which is what we refer to today as "Israel."

The history and development of the Jewish people during the period leading up to the destruction and exile is narrated through the books of Samuel and Kings. The books endorse and support the superiority of the priests called Cohanim. Little is said about those who were called Levites. But that changed when the country that Saul created, David solidified, and where Solomon built a central place of worship, became divided into two countries.

THE DEVELOPMENT OF NORTHERN ISRAELITE RELIGION

In 928 B.C.E., Solomon's son Rehoboam was abandoned by the ten northern tribes leaving him with the tribes of Benjamin and Judah who had settled in the South. Ten tribes supposedly peacefully seceded from the union and for the next several hundred years were referred to as either "Israel," "Ephraim" or "Samaria", while the southern ones, Judah and Benjamin, were referred to as" Judah."

Jerusalem was in the province of Judah. Judah, after all wasn't just a tribe, the Judahites were descendants of the leader of Jacob's sons. Judah was the son who saved his brother Joseph's life by selling him to the Midianites. Judah was the son who years later negotiated with Joseph and refused to give up his youngest brother Benjamin. Jewish history from a biblical point of view can be understood as the history of the tribe of Judah.

The book of 1 Kings portrays Reheboam as being ill advised and attempting to rule both the north and the south with an iron hand.

> *"My father chastised you with whips, but I will chastise you with scorpions.*
> (1 Kings 12:11)

While that might have been one of the reasons the split occurred, it was also encouraged by the current ruler of Egypt, Shishak. Shishak supported one of Solomon's former employees and encouraged him to lead a rebellion. His name was Jeroboam.

At one time Jeroboam was in charge of Solomon's forced labor crews that were building the Temple in Jerusalem. We are told (1 Kings 11:30-31) that the prophet Ahijah foretold that ten of the twelve tribes would be taken from the descendants of Solomon and given to him. Solomon's response to this prophecy was to issue a death warrant for Jeroboam. This forced him to flee to Egypt where he remained until Solomon's death. Then, with the backing of Shishak, he returned and led a successful revolt against Rehoboam attracting all of the tribes with the exception of Benjamin and Judah.

The process of creating a country is complicated. In Jeroboam's case it was further complicated because the religious center of the nation was in Jerusalem which was, of course, in Judah. In order for his country to truly become independent he needed to provide a place and format for his people to worship.

Jeroboam created two religious centers. He placed one on the northern border and one even farther north on the slopes of Mount Harmon. The first site, Beth El, the place where Jacob had his vision of a ladder reaching up to heaven, was twelve miles north of Jerusalem. The second site was a Canaanite city north of the Sea of Galilee called Laish. He renamed it Dan. Jeroboam had golden calves erected at each of these sites and had them ministered by his own Levitical priesthood who were descended from Moses (Judges 18:30). Golden calves? Why did he make that decision?

Many of the priests, let's call them the descendants of Levi, had been ministering to religious sites in the territories of the northern tribes since the time of the Judges. In their own way they were just as legitimate as the priests who were serving in the Temple.

The nation called "Israel 2" continued to develop and its rulers formed strategic alliances with neighboring nations. As a result of an alliance with the country (city-state) of Tyre, an Israelite king married a priestess of Baal. Her name was Jezebel. She also introduced or at least made the worship of her god, Baal, along with its rights acceptable in the northern court.

The introduction of Baal worship stimulated an aggressive response by the prophets of Yahweh, led by Elijah and Elisha which challenged Jewish religion to become more theologically sophisticated. Elijah and Elisha inspired a military coup against the northern monarchs, the Omrides.

The struggle against Baal continued in the North in the eighth century B.C.E. guided by the prophet Hosea. Hosea was one of the first of the poetic prophets. He introduced the metaphor of Israel being likened to an adulterous wife who has worshipped other gods but would be forgiven in the same way that an adulterous wife who strayed from her husband would be forgiven. I have some serious doubts about that, but if one believes in

God, anything is possible.

If you're a Levite or know someone who is a Levite, take a moment and explain to them that way back when, they weren't second class priests but representatives of a different tradition, one that began to have a huge impact on modern Jewish life before the destruction of the First Temple during the time of King Josiah.

And you will learn more about that in the story that follows.

And this is their story:

THE LEVITICAL PRIESTS WERE DIFFERENT FROM THE *COHANIM*

While the Levites seem to have second class status today (and it is true that egalitarianism in the non-Orthodox world is rapidly overshadowing priestly recognition), their importance and their impact on the development of Jewish life and Judaism for the past several thousand years should not be forgotten or masked. Since it doesn't seem logical that they should be recognized solely on the basis of their genealogy, we need to dig deeper for an explanation.

The Levites were part of the priestly tribe descended from the third son of Jacob whose name was Levi. According to the books of Exodus, Leviticus and Numbers the Levites had specific duties during Temple times. Their main job was to assist the priests called *Cohanim*. Today the *Cohanim* receive the first *aliyah* to the Torah, and can bestow the priestly blessing upon the congregation. They are not supposed to come in contact with the dead or to marry a divorcee. In addition, the first born male child of a *Cohen* technically belongs to God and needs to be redeemed by another *Cohen* on the thirtieth day after his birth.

The rules are different for a *Levi*. They aren't redeemed by a *Cohen* and they don't bless the people. Instead, they wash the *Cohen's* hands and feet so he can bless the people. It seems that *Levi'im* weren't and haven't been very important. But they were.

They were a group of people who most probably helped instill in the Jewish people the commitment to interpret and study the Law. Some of them also had great musical talents. Unfortunately, their message and importance has been lost.

How did it all begin?

Jochebed, Levi's daughter gave birth to three children: Miriam, Aaron, and Moses. Aaron was the first high priest *(Cohen)*. When he died Moses transferred his authority and position to his son Eleazar. Eleazar was succeeded by his son Phineas.

According to the Torah, when the twelve tribes entered the land of Israel, the priests, both the descendants of Aaron and the larger clan of Levi from which they descended, were not permitted to own property because they were considered to be servants of God. Wherever they settled in this new land they found places to worship and most likely built altars or temples. There were a number of holy places: Shechem, Shiloh and Mitzpeh were just a few. The *haftarah* that is read on the first morning of Rosh Hashanah tells the story of the birth of the prophet, judge and kingmaker Samuel which takes place at Shiloh.

The priesthood became institutionalized when King Solomon built the Temple in Jerusalem and Hebrew writing came into being. In this newly formed nation, priestly skills and knowledge were needed in a number of areas. The priests offered sacrifices on a regular basis and most likely kept financial records. One priest, by the name of Zadok became King David's priest. His descendants remained as High Priests until they were overthrown by the Maccabees one thousand years later.

King David centralized the government in Jerusalem and his son Solomon built the Temple and institutionalized the High Priesthood. These priests and their descendants came to be called, *Cohanim*. The priests who operated outside of Jerusalem came to be called, or always were called, *Levi'im*.

Solomon had many children but the one who inherited his throne was named Reheboam. According to the Bible, he was either a harsh man or one that was poorly advised, because in order to become king, he was forced to transfer the coronation ceremony from Jerusalem to Shechem. That would be like the president of the United States being inaugurated in Chicago, Dallas, or Poughkeepsie, instead of Washington.

The inauguration didn't go very well and ten of the twelve tribes seceded from the union. This occurred in response to Reheboam's threat to raise taxes and to increase the military draft. The tribes were adjusting to being part of a new country and were seeking leniency and a just and understanding king. When they heard Reheboam's inaugural address they left. The land surrounding Jerusalem came to be called Judah, and the land governed by the ten tribes who had left the union from this point onward was referred to as either Israel or Ephraim.

The secession was led by a man named Jeroboam who was a former soldier in Solomon's army. The Bible informs us that Solomon was impressed with his competency and leadership. Unfortunately for him, he was critical of some of Solomon's policies and as a result was forced to flee to Egypt in order to preserve his life.

As soon as Solomon died Jeroboam returned and was embraced as a leader of the Northern tribes. While the circumstances surrounding how he achieved this position of authority are not totally clear, he was acknowledged as the first King of the ten northern tribes. The book of Kings initially paints Jeroboam as an ideal leader who is likened to King David, but that's another story.

As the leader of new country, Jeroboam was challenged to create both a viable government and an acceptable religion. This was difficult because the place where they had been worshipping, that is to say, offering sacrifices to the Lord when Solomon was king, was in Jerusalem.

The ancient traditions and holy places dating back to the people's entrée into the land still remained and probably hadn't been abandoned. Jeroboam established two Temples, built golden calves for the purpose of worship and installed his own priesthood. This priesthood remained the priests of the Kings for almost two hundred years, that is, until the Northern Kingdom was destroyed by the Assyrian empire in 721 B.C.E.

In anticipation of the pending destruction many of the Levites migrated south and took up residence in Jerusalem. The Kings of Judah (Jerusalem) most likely acknowledged their distant relatives and accorded them some form of priestly status. They were accepted as priests but were not permitted to offer sacrifices in the Temple.

One hundred years later a man named, Josiah became King of Judah. One of the things he did was to successfully unite Judah and Israel. He also re-organized the country. There is a story in 2 Kings which describes some of his activities.

2 Kings 22 informs us that during his reign an ancient book was discovered in the Temple and as a result of its contents Josiah re-organized the country. He abolished the local places of worships and made everyone acknowledge Jerusalem and the Temple as the only place sacrifice could occur. He combined a festival of unleavened bread and a festival of freedom into the Passover festival we celebrate today and he replaced the local system of governance by the elders of a community with the Levites who served as his government representatives. He empowered the Levites to travel throughout the country and to gain acceptance of his new way of governing. They were entrusted with instituting and interpreting the law, most of which can be found in the book of Deuteronomy.

Twenty four years later, Nebuchadnezzar, the King of Babylon conquered Israel and forcibly exiled the aristocracy, priesthood and what we would call today, the intelligentsia of Israel, to a suburb of Babylon called Nippur. It was 597 B.C.E. He had his reasons, but suffice it to say, as a result of the actions of the people who remained in power in Jerusalem, he returned thirteen years later and destroyed the Temple.

When we think of exile we understand it to be a negative distressing ordeal. I suppose the initial deportation was difficult and it most likely took some time for the exiles to adjust to their new surroundings. But they weren't enslaved. They weren't persecuted and in fact they integrated very readily into a larger more urban society.

Babylon was a sophisticated and prosperous empire, and the new immigrants, like many of our grandparents and great grandparents who came to this new country, this new land of opportunity, worked very hard to adapt and integrate.

Most of them already knew the language; Babylonian was spoken throughout the ancient near east, much like English is spoken throughout Europe. Our ancestors, adopted Babylonian names, like Mordecai and Esther; they changed the names of the months of the calendar. In their tradition the months' names were first month, second month and so on. Our ancestors in Babylon selected new names for the month, names like Kislev, or Adar, or Tishrei. That's right; the names of the months in the Hebrew calendar have Babylonian origins.

Life was good in Babel. Within a generation people found employment as traders, craftsmen, scribes, musicians and some even became government and officials, like Mordecai in the Esther-Purim story. It was during this time that the Levites and the *Cohanim* crafted the Torah.

Fifty years later, a new emperor named Cyrus, permitted the exiles to return to Jerusalem and to begin rebuilding the Temple. He made it easy; he provided them with money and tax exemptions. Of course, everyone didn't want to return. Life was so good in Babylon.

It took a long time for the Temple to be rebuilt. There were work stoppages and all sorts of political intrigues, but eventually it happened. The completion of the Temple was the next step in the evolution of the Jewish people and in 459 B.C.E. a Cohen named Ezra traveled from Babylon with soldiers and musicians, and some say prophets, but others say Levites, to Jerusalem. He carried with him a scroll that had been compiled by *Cohanim* and *Levi'im* that told the story of the Jewish people. This scroll, which we call the Torah, became the source of inspiration from that time until this very day.

For the next few hundred years, Levites taught the laws and the interpretation of those laws to the Jewish people. They taught in Israel and in Egypt and in Greece and wherever Jewish people lived. The Levites had status. Local rulers called upon them to settle legal disputes and to make peace between conflicted parties. They were the lawyers, judges and arbitrators all rolled into one.

Eventually, many of them came to be called *sofrim* or scribes. Scribes in those days did a lot more than scribes do today. They didn't just copy texts or write letters, they interpreted the Law.

While the Levites taught, judged and interpreted, the *Cohanim* presided over the sacrificial system and often served as the liaisons for the Jewish people to foreign rulers. Judah and Israel, one country or two were almost always subject to a foreign authority and the High priest in Jerusalem almost always served as its representative to the ruling power. They were supported by the Levites who were not permitted to offer sacrifices in Jerusalem.

Some people believe that the descendants of the scribes morphed into the political party called the Pharisees. The Pharisees after the Second Temple was destroyed became what today are referred to as rabbis.

During the time leading up to the Second Temple's destruction and most likely through the fourth century C.E., many of our customs developed, one of which was that the Levi was called to the Torah after the *Cohen*.

Unlike the impression we have today, the Levites, the so-called second class priests, were much more important than we realize. To a great extent they were the creators of our intellectual traditions. Originally they traveled from one place to another and eventually in time, they settled, purchased land and lived in the community. During that time they were viewed as the people who explained and interpreted God's law.

That means they were understood to be the intermediaries between heaven and earth, the physical and the meta-physical, the holiness and the spiritual.

An early translation of the book of Nehemiah substitutes the word *Levi* for prophet. So think about this if you're a *Levi,* or the daughter of a *Levi:* you are an inheritor of the most important document that shaped the history of the Jewish people. What your ancestors began evolved into a commitment to study, a commitment to fostering intellectual curiosity and much more.

If you're a *Levi,* remember this, be proud of it, and teach it to your children.

THE TRAGEDY OF KING SAUL

A DEMOCRAT IN A REPUBLICAN CONGRESS

Like Macbeth, Saul (1079 -1007 B.C.E.) was a tragic hero unable to rise to the occasion to become fully successful. From the beginning of his monarchy when the prophet Samuel selected him, through his rise to power and ultimate demise, the Bible casts him in a way that belies what I think is more the political reality he confronted. Regardless of which party or candidate one chooses to favor today, the title of this section reflects what I believe is a more effective way to understand and relate to Saul and the challenges he faced. At the same time, his story offers us an opportunity to broaden our understanding of the forces which could have shaped the text. And, it gives us the opportunity of a different context in which to consider the choices we make or which are imposed upon us by others.

WHY AND HOW WAS THIS KING ANOINTED?

Saul was chosen and anointed as king by Samuel. Samuel, as far as we know, was the only person in ancient Israel who could have accomplished this task. The only other way to become king was for a man to create an army and forcibly conquer the surrounding lands. Samuel was able to achieve his goal, according to the text, because he was the major religious and secular leader of the time. He embodied each of the three major institutions or offices of the day. He was the last of the judges and as such, was called upon to resolve disputes. He was a prophet and heard the voice of God. And he was a priest who had been trained at the place where the Ark of the Covenant primarily resided, Shiloh. It is likely that because he held all three of these offices and in light of the Philistine incursion which demanded a united defense, he quite literally rose to the position of king-maker. In that role, he anointed both Saul and his successor, David.

It is generally accepted that a monarchy was needed in Israel in order to preserve the nation against the Philistine incursion, and because the people, at least some of the people, desired a king…to be like other nations.

All the elders of Israel assembled and came to Samuel at Ramah, and they said to him, "You have grown old and your sons have not followed your ways. Therefore appoint a king for us, to govern us like all other nations." (1 Samuel 8:4-5)

Yet at the same time the text is ambivalent because it acknowledges that God is King.

Samuel was displeased that they said, "Give us a king to govern us." Samuel prayed to the Lord and the Lord replied to Samuel, "Heed the demand of the people in everything they say to you. For it is not you that they rejected; it is Me that they have rejected as their king. Heed their demand; but warn them solemnly, and tell them about the practices of any king who will rule over them." (1 Samuel 8:6-9)

This theological statement could reflect the philosophy of a group of people who did not favor the establishment of a monarchy. While they might claim to speak or interpret for God, their reasons for not supporting a monarch are obvious. They feared the loss of their independence and the subjugation of their rights to a governing body. They realized that a strong government would result in increased taxes, and they understood that a strong king would create an army thus placing their sons at risk and depriving local villages of a needed labor force.

He will take your sons and appoint them as his charioteers and horsemen, and they will serve as out runners for his chariots. He will take your daughters as perfumers, cooks and bakers. He will seize your choice fields, vineyards and olive groves and give them to his courtiers. He will take a tenth part of your grain and vintage and give it to his eunuchs and courtiers. He will take your male and females slaves, your choice young men and your asses and put them to work for him. He will take a tenth part of you flock and you shall become his slaves. (1 Samuel 8:11-18)

This group, let's call them the opposition, might have favored people being governed by a tribal chiefdom based on the status quo, rather than empowering someone to lead a nation.

Samuel's selection of Saul seemed to reflect this ambivalence. Saul was the son of Kish from the tribe of Benjamin. Benjamin was the weakest of the tribes, one which had been dependent upon the good will of the tribal confederacy just a few years back.

> And on the third day, the Israelites went up against the Benjaminites, and engaged them in battle at Gibeah. That day the Israelites, slew 25,100 men of Benjamin, all of them fighting men…the total number of Benjaminites who feel that day came to 25,00 fighting men, all of them brave. (Judges 20:30 – 21:25)

It causes one to wonder why one of the stronger tribes didn't field a candidate. Surprisingly, or not, his candidacy received support, endorsements, from two of the most powerful groups at the time, Judah in the south and Ephraim in the north. Imagine that, the two most powerful groups in ancient Israel selected a leader from a tribe that couldn't pose a threat to their authority and relied upon their beneficence for support!

One can understand why two powerful groups would favor a weaker party but were there any other groups who would also oppose the creation of a strong monarchy? Consider Samuel and the priestly faction. He realized the need for a king but also had reason to desire a king who could be guided, or controlled. Samuel was raised in the village of Shiloh and spoke for the priesthood which controlled one of the few religious, holy, artifacts of early Israelite religion. Like others he could have been fearful of having his authority and the authority of the priesthood, the only remaining institution in Israel at the time that had any credibility, diminished or usurped. When Saul acted too independently, the text continues:

> Go attack Amalek spare no-one kill alike all men and women infants and cows, oxen and sheep, camels and asses! (1 Samuel 15:3)
> Saul destroyed Amalek…but spared Agag and the best of the sheep, the oxen, the second-born, the lambs, and all else that was of value… (1 Samuel 15:9)

Samuel's response was to revoke his Kingship. Imagine that! It's like revoking the bar mitzvah of a man and turning him once again into a boy.

> *For rebellion is like the sin of divination, Defiance, like the iniquity of teraphim. Because you rejected the Lord's command, He has rejected you as king.* (1 Samuel 15:23)

Samuel hadn't left his country ruler-less; he had just withdrawn his support. He needed a replacement. Imagine that, Saul remained king while his mentor actively campaigned against him. At this point the text informs us that God guided Samuel's selection of Saul's successor, David.

The text explained it this way, that the spirit of the Lord had departed from Saul and an evil spirit began to terrify him. Consider how you might feel if you were waging war on a number of fronts and your mentor was actively campaigning against you? Would you feel a little bit threatened? Perhaps even a little bit jealous after David conquered Goliath? Once again the text reflects different opinions. On one hand, Saul finds David's presence and musical ability comforting. On the other hand David's military successes force Saul to give his daughter to him as a wife thus practically announcing him as his successor. In the meantime David's continued successes increased Saul's anxiety.

There are a number of reasons why David succeeded. Unlike Saul, David maintained a private army while Saul relied upon volunteers and lacked sufficient authority to create a draft. This situation only exacerbated the tensions between them. In addition to having cobbled together a private army, making him kind of a Robin Hood type figure, David was the first king of Israel to engage in public relations. He promoted himself and thus further undermined the king.

The story of David's relationship with Saul's first son, Jonathan and his relationship to Saul's second daughter and his first wife, Michal, will be told in a bit; when you read the text you can see good public relations at work. The way his public relations employee described David's character, even when he was being hunted by Saul and his army, is explained in the first book of Samuel. But this isn't a tale about David. It's about Israel's first king and the forces that shaped him.

QUESTIONS? LESSONS?

The story of Saul his strengths and weaknesses, his successes and failures, reflect the struggles of a person who wasn't up to the job. But it wasn't necessarily his fault. Careful analysis of his story seems to indicate that he was chosen to serve as king precisely because he couldn't fully succeed. This causes one to wonder how often lofty goals and ideals are thwarted because people in positions of influence lack the greater vision and are loathe to cede any authority or influence to others. It causes one to wonder how we would react if we were the people at risk of losing what we had. And hopefully, it challenges us to rethink positions that maintain the status quo and take a risk for the greater good.

Section 2

DAVID THE KING
Fables & Foibles

INTRODUCTION

The story of David, a simple shepherd who became a king and united a country, has been depicted in art and literature for approximately 2,600 years. He allegedly lived in the tenth century B.C.E., and established Jerusalem (aka the city of David) as its country's capital; he is referred to as "the ideal king", the one whom God loved the most. A musician, a poet, and according to legend the author of a number of Psalms, he is the progenitor of the Messiah. Yet when we study the stories that are transmitted to us in the Bible, we see a totally different picture.

The David of the Bible is described over and over again as a man ruled by his passions who continually errs. Early in his career he demonstrates a noble character and a deep abiding faith. However, as the years passed and life became more complicated, the high ideals to which he had aspired were replaced by more basic, selfish desires. What follows are a series of stories from the Bible, each describing David from a different vantage point at a various stages in his life. (Whether they actually occurred is not relevant here.) The family relationships are important because they shed light on ancient court life in the Middle East which is not too different from life in modern-day Iraq, Iran, and Saudi Arabia.

The incidents recorded in the text were transmitted orally from the time they occurred until they were written down hundreds of years later. Undoubtedly they were edited by authors who wished to resolve tensions between the northern Israelite and southern Judean cultures in order to provide the people of the time with a national identity. Beginning with the familiar story of David and Goliath, we will uncover what I believe was the message the authors intended to convey.

As you read the rest of the tales in this section, consider why David, in spite of all of his foibles, was so loved by God and what lesson if any, is meant to be conveyed. There will be specific questions after each to help guide you.

DAVID AND GOLIATH

THE STORY OF DAVID AND GOLIATH

The victory of David over Goliath is one of the most memorable scenes in the Bible and is part of a major saga which shaped the Western world. The story is so intrinsic to our tradition, that we could say that if Goliath had beaten and killed David that the history of Israel and the Jewish people would never have occurred. There wouldn't be a holy city and our hopes for a messiah would never have developed.

According to the Bible it took place sometime around the year 950 B.C.E. Its reflections, like ripples in a pond, have been mirrored in art, literature, and in comparisons of kings in Judaism, Christianity and Islam. Because it so closely resembles the mythic duels between Greek and Trojan heroes, it helps explain why it has become such a powerful influence in the Western world. Did it really happen? Does that matter? What are the messages that it sends?

1 Samuel 17: 1-51 tells the story - but first a little background.

The Philistines are the main antagonists in the books of Judges and Samuel. A number of other encounters between the children of Israel and the Philistines occurred prior to David's meeting with Goliath. They were routed by Saul's son Jonathan at Michmesh and they captured the Ark of the Covenant and defeated King Saul at the battle of Aphek. Following that they were once again defeated at Ebenezer. David's story begins following their defeat and prior to the battle at Mount Gilboa where Saul and his sons were killed.

Saul and the men of Israel had massed and encamped in the valley of Elah. (The valley of Elah is approximately 45 minutes southwest of Jerusalem and today is the rising star of Israel's wine industry.) They drew up their lines of battle against the Philistines. The Philistines stationed themselves on one hill and Israel stationed itself on the one opposite.

A champion of the Philistine forces named Goliath of Gath stepped forward. Apparently Gath, which was one of the five major Philistine cities, produced tall men because Goliath wasn't the only Philistine giant described in the books of Samuel.

We are told that:

> *Ishbi-benob, one of the descendants of the giants, whose spear weighed three hundred shekels of bronze and who was girded with a new sword, sought to kill David, but Abishai son of Zeruiah came to his aid and attacked the Philistine and killed him.* (2 Samuel 21:16-17)

> *And there was a man of great stature who had six fingers on each hand, and six toes on each foot, twenty-four in number; and he was also descended from the giants. And when he taunted Israel, Jonathon the son of Shimei, David's brother slew him.* (2 Samuel 21:20-21)

And finally and most problematically:

> *...there was again a war with the Philistines at Gob and Elhanan the son of Jaare-oregim, the Bethlehemite, slew Goliath of Gath, the shaft of whose spear was like a weaver's beam.* (2 Samuel 21:19)

Was this a coincidence that a man with a different name from the same birthplace as David slew a giant named Goliath? Did a tradition of a man killing a giant exist prior to our story's being recorded? It doesn't matter because the story was crafted to be told.

Goliath was six cubits and a span almost nine feet tall. Josephus and the Dead Sea scrolls record a different tradition which claimed he was only four cubits and a bit, which would make him about 6' 9", but that's still a pretty big guy and the average height of man who lived three thousand years ago likely wasn't more than five feet.

Goliath wore a bronze helmet and a breastplate of scale armor, weighing five thousand shekels, approximately 155 pounds. He had bronze greaves on his legs and a bronze javelin strung across his shoulders. The shaft of his spear was like a weaver's bar, and the iron head of his spear weighted six hundred shekels; around eighteen pounds.

To be clear, this was not what we know as tenth century B.C.E. Philistine armor; on the contrary it was armor that reflected the Greek culture of the sixth century B.C.E. Why would the author or authors of this story tell the story utilizing the language and culture of a people who lived four hundred years after the incident allegedly took place?

Goliath stepped forward so all the Israelites could see him and he called out to the ranks of Israel,

> *Why should you come out to engage in battle? I am the Philistine (champion) and you are Saul's servants. Choose one of your men and let him come against me. If he beats me in combat and kills me, we will become your slaves, but if I best him and kill him, you shall be our slaves and serve us.*

> *I defy you Israel, get me a man and let's fight it out*

When Saul and all Israel heard these words they were terror stricken and every morning and evening for the forty days Goliath challenged the army of Israel.

One could surmise the Philistines didn't want to attack because they didn't want to relinquish their strategic location on the mountain or they were unsure themselves because Saul's son, Jonathan, had defeated them when they last met.

One could also surmise the Israelites didn't want to relinquish their strategic advantage and they were afraid of this giant of a man. Saul could not have been confident of victory.

Enter David, the son of a certain Ephrathite of Bethlehem in Judah whose name was Jesse. Jesse had eight sons, the three oldest had gone to fight in the war with Saul. David was the youngest and as the youngest his job was to go back and forth between Saul and his father and to serve as a shepherd for his father's flock.

One day, Jesse told David to:

Take an ephah of parched corn and carry it quickly to your brothers in camp. And take these ten cheeses to the captain of their thousand. Find out how your brothers are doing and bring me back something of that belongs to them so I know that they have not come to harm.

Early the next morning, David put someone in charge of the flock, and took the grain and cheese as his father had instructed him. He reached the barricade as the army was going out to the battle lines shouting the war cry. David watched Israel and the Philistines draw up their battle lines one opposite the other and then he saw one of his brothers. He left his baggage with the man in charge of baggage and ran toward the battle line to greet his brothers.

While he was talking to them, the champion Goliath, the Philistine of Gath, stepped forward and repeated the same challenge that he had been doing morning and night. When the men of Israel saw him they fled in terror.

David turned to one of the men standing near him and asked:

Who is that uncircumcised Philistine that dares defy the ranks of the living God and what reward will the man who slays him receive?

The man told him that Saul will reward whoever kills Goliath with great riches, his daughter in marriage and tax exemption for his father's house.

At this point, Eliab, David's oldest brother overheard this conversation and became angry with David and said:

Why did you come down here, and with whom did you leave those few sheep in the wilderness? I know your impudence and your impertinence; you came here to watch the fighting!

And David replied:

What have I done now? I was only asking! He turned away from his brother and asked the same questions to others. Each time he asked he received the same answer as before.

After a while word of this questioning boy was reported to Saul and Saul sent for him. The text doesn't tell us if any small talk occurred. All it relates is that David said to Saul:

Let no man's courage fail him. I will fight that Philistine." And Saul replied, "You can't go and fight him, you are just a boy and Goliath is a giant who has been a warrior from his youth.

David replied with strong words to the King:

I have been tending my father's sheep, and if a lion or a bear carried off an animal from the flock, I would go after it and fight and rescue it from its mouth. And if it attacked me, I would seize it by the beard and strike it down and kill it. I have killed lions and bears and that uncircumcised Philistine shall end up like one of them, for he has defied the ranks of the living God. The Lord, who saved me from lion and bear will also save me from that Philistine.

Could it be that the skills David learned as a shepherd fighting off lions and bears had prepared him to fight Goliath? It's true he has learned how to kill and most likely use some sort of weapon, which might have been more than some of the men in Saul's volunteer army, but could he kill a giant?

Saul must have been having a bad day or David evinced but another sign of his inability to lead, because he permits David to represent his army, his nation.

Shouldn't he have considered the consequences? What would have happened if David had lost?

Then Saul said to David: Go and may the Lord be with you.

Imagine how humiliated or terror stricken Saul must have been. For forty days and forty nights he failed to act and instead lived in fear, and now a young confident man approaches him and offers to perform an unimaginable act and he acquiesces.

He clothed David with his own garments. He placed his bronze helmet on his head and fastened a breastplate on him. He gave David his sword. And it was too much!

David tried to walk but could barely move. So he took them off and took his stick and picked a few smooth stones from the wadi, placed them in the pocket of his shepherd's bag and, sling in hand, he went to meet Goliath.

Meanwhile, Goliath and his shield-bearer began to approach David. When he finally saw him, he looked at this handsome and ruddy boy and scornfully called out to David,

> *Am I a dog that you come against me with sticks?" He cursed David by his Gods, and said, "All right boy, come here and I will give your flesh to the birds of the sky and the beasts of the field.*

And David replied,

> *You come against me with a sword, spear and a javelin; but I approach you in the name of the Lord of Hosts, the God of the ranks of Israel, whom you have defied. This very day the Lord will deliver you into my hands. I will kill you and cut off your head; and I will give 'the carcasses' of the Philistine camp to the birds of the sky and the beasts of the earth. All the earth shall know that there is a God in Israel. And the whole assembly shall know that the Lord can give victory without sword or spear. For the battle is in the Lord's and He will deliver you into our hands.*

Goliath drew closer to him and David turned to face him. He put his hand into the bag; took out a stone and slung it. It struck and sank into Goliath's forehead and he fell face down on the ground. David approached him, stood over him and grasped Goliath's sword and pulled it from its sheath. And then he cut off his head. David took Goliath's head and brought it to Jerusalem.

And thus David bested the Philistines with sling and stone and killed him without a sword.

Jerusalem, his destined city. Imagine, prior to establishing Jerusalem as his capital, David carries Goliath's head with him to show its inhabitants. It could have been the head of a bear or a lion that had stolen his sheep, but our authors have him bring the head of his enemy to his destined city to demonstrate that he would protect his people like a shepherd protects his flock.

The authors of this story had to have lived in Homeric times because that was when Goliath's armor, the javelin and leg greaves, came into use. They could have told the story without it and it still would have been a story about a man of faith defeating a giant. But the story's authors weren't necessarily telling a story about David. They were imparting to the reader a vision of a small nation that had been living in exile within the giant's territory. Let's call this territory Babylon. And they wished that those exiles, our ancestors, would have the faith to believe that God would assist them in their battle to return to their promised land. They drew upon legends of past heroes to encourage their people to believe, to have faith. That's one of the messages of the story of David and Goliath.

After killing Goliath, David became a national hero and Saul became in-surmountably jealous of David's success. David, fearing for his life, flees to an area south of Jerusalem which is referred to as the "wilderness." A wilderness with which he was familiar since it was close to the place he had been raised.

He attracted a band of men to his side. Men who weren't the noblest of sorts. The book of Samuel informs us they were the poor, the discontent, and those who had been cast out. All of a sudden, or so it seems, David had his own private army and Saul had reason to be fearful. David was an adept leader. As chief of a local band of men he fended off enemy attacks, settled disagreements, and distributed captured plunder to the poor and oppressed.

At first he attracted forty men. Over time and as a result of his successful activities his band grew to two hundred. From two hundred to four hundred and from four hundred to six hundred.

Over time the people began to tell stories about his victories. Perhaps they embellished them a little bit, as we tend to do with our own family stories. Eventually these and heroic tales were transmuted into songs. Over time, lots of time, those songs spawned legends.

The story of the youth who killed the giant blossomed. He gathered an army, became king, expanded his nation from the Egyptian border to the Euphrates and over time morphed into an image of the ideal king, poet, man of action and man of faith. As the story grew, David emerged as the one whom God loved the most, the recipient of the fulfillment of God's promise to Abraham and the progenitor of the Messiah.

But David was not blameless. One can perhaps hear a bit of arrogance in his voice prior to the battle with Goliath or perhaps it was just the confidence of a man with a mission. Unfortunately, David's success brought with it, like it does with each of us, a host of complications. The more we engage with others, especially if we are placed in positions of authority, the more complicated our lives become.

During the period of his life when fleeing from Saul, he was forced to collaborate with the Philistines. As he aided villages under attack and/or distributed items of value that he had gained from plundering caravans, he actively undermined Saul's authority.

David's confidence and skill might have led him to reach for the golden ring and become king. But once that goal had been achieved his life was fraught with danger. Was it the power of kingship that overshadowed and conquered the belief and strength of the boy who had once heard God's voice and conquered a giant?

Was it a coincidence that almost all of Saul's family and closest associates were assassinated as soon as David became King?

Of course he immediately disavowed any responsibility, but as soon as he consolidated his power he became infatuated with Bathsheba and deliberately arranged her husband's death. This is the darker side of our hero.

As he aged, he became increasingly powerless and failed to address the rivalry among his children. At the end of his life, he is pictured as an impotent old man, unable to address the needs of the time and constantly manipulated by his family.

The messages of the authors challenge us on many levels. It encourages us to be a people who believe that giants can be conquered. For a nation that existed in the sixth century B.C.E., a nation conquered by a giant of Babylonian nature, it offered hope that just as an ancient hero of old overcame tremendous obstacles and triumphed because of his faith that Israel could once again hear God's voice and would be re-established once again.

The story of the rise of a young hero, a warrior and a man of confidence and faith who replaces a failed leader and over time became the embodiment of his people's hopes and dreams is one of the classic myths of the

Western world. David and his son Solomon are revered as the greatest leaders of God's chosen kingdom. They were the recipients of a divine promise that Israel would become a great nation, a promise that ensured the survival and eventual redemption of the Jewish people.

But, what other messages do we glean from this story?

It is possible that initially David heard God's voice but as his life became more complicated and he aged his vision of the person he would like to become changed. Does David's story challenge us to remember our early visions of who we would like to become?

I find it remarkable that the story's authors shaped our love and attachment to Jerusalem. Do we have similar, though of course on a smaller scale, master stories that we wish to share with emerging generations?

LOVE'S LABORS LOST

Michal, Daughter of Saul

(1 Samuel 18:17-26; 1 Samuel 19; 2 Samuel 3:11-14)

One of the most misrepresented and maligned people in the Bible, second only to Manasseh, is Saul's daughter Michal. She is briefly mentioned in the haftarah (prophetic portion) which is read in conjunction with the Torah portion titled Shmini (Leviticus 9-11) in a most unflattering light.

We are told that David, after having survived for political reasons, suffered a failed attempt to bring the Ark of the Covenant to Jerusalem, an act which weakened him considerably. After an extended period of time, he was able to recoup and regroup and successfully manage to have the Ark transported to Jerusalem in a royal manner.

He began the Ark's journey dressed in fine linens with the ephod, another object of religious significance, hanging from his neck. This was followed by appropriate sacrifices and supplemented with an army shouting, most likely singing for joy, while being accompanied by the blasts of horns. Upon entering the city, he began to leap and dance and whirl before the Lord.

And the text informs us that Michal, his first wife, saw him performing in this manner and despised him.

Wait a minute!

Why would David's wife despise her husband after witnessing a magnificent public performance worthy of a great king? After all, he didn't do this lightly. This was a serious undertaking.

First he organized a huge parade.

Then upon entering the city he offered a series of public sacrifices. Following that he blessed all of the people in the name of the Lord.

Finally, as a token of his joy he distributed a goody-bag to each man and woman containing a loaf of bread, a cake and a special cake made with raisins.

This was a serious event that took a great deal of planning. It was a pageant and yet the Bible tells us that upon returning home his wife said,

> *Didn't the king of Israel do himself honor today-exposing himself in the sight of the slave girls of his subjects, and appearing as one of the riffraff might expose himself!*

Did he deserve this type of response? Were celebratory actions worthy of such disdain? I know that if I successfully pulled off an event as complex and politically charged as this one, my wife would have been more than supportive. She would have been proud.

Was Michal so petty a person that the way her husband behaved in public warranted such a negative response?

David's response was also perplexing. Okay, his feelings were bruised but was that a sufficient reason not to sleep with her and to leave her barren for the rest of her life?

> *It was before the Lord who chose me instead of our father and all his family and appointed me ruler over the Lord's people Israel! I will dance before the Lord and dishonor myself even more, and be low in my own esteem; but among slave girls that you speak of I will be honored. So to her dying day Michal daughter of Saul had no children.*

And we never hear about Michal again.

Doesn't this entire scenario appear to be a little extreme? After all how many husbands and wives don't fight? Are there any? What could have occurred during the time of their marriage that caused David to respond and to act with such venom? What could have transpired to cause him to harbor so much hate such an intense dislike that he refused to be intimate with her ever again?

Or, could it be that there is more to the story of David and Michal? Might there be reasons that influenced the authors of this text to present the story the way it has been preserved? Let's examine what the text tells us about Michal and her relationship with David and see what really might have caused their not-so-little marital dispute.

Michal was Saul's second daughter. Saul and Samuel had recently had a falling out leaving Saul without an advisor. The pressure must have been terrible. The Philistines were attacking on several fronts and Saul was forced to rely upon a volunteer army. When David entered the scene following his victory over Goliath, Saul was already experiencing fits of depression. He or someone near him engaged David, the musician, to help Saul remain calm.

David was already established as a hero, and as such posed a threat to Saul's authority and possible plans for a successor. By rights, David should have been betrothed to his oldest daughter. But Saul was cautious and a little paranoid.

He said to David: "Here is my older daughter, Merab; I will give her to you in marriage; in return, you will be my warrior and fight the battles of the Lord" ....But at the time that Merab, daughter of Saul, should have been given to David; was given to Adriel the Meholathite.

By betrothing his second daughter to David, he placed an obstacle to succession in front of David.

Enter Michal.

Now Michal, daughter of Saul had fallen in love with David.

Seeking to capitalize on this Saul offered him his daughter, once removed from the throne, on condition that David had to kill one hundred Philistines.

...and when this was reported to Saul, he was pleased. Saul thought, I will give her to him, and she can serve as a snare for him, so that the Philistines may kill him.

Unfortunately for Saul and fortunately for David, defeating Philistines was a piece of cake and David's reputation grew.

Saul has slain thousands; David, his tens of thousands.

When Saul realized that the Lord was with David and that Michael loved him he grew more afraid of David; and Saul was David's enemy ever after.

But Michal loved her husband and was loyal to him.

That night, Saul sent messengers to David's home to keep watch on him and to kill him in the morning. But David's wife Michal told him, "Unless you run for your life tonight, you will be killed tomorrow". Michal let David down from the window and he escaped and fled.

Michal then took the house old idol, laid it on the bed, covered it with cloth; and at its head but a net of goat's hair. Saul sent messengers to seize David, but she said, "He is sick". Saul sent back the messengers and ordered them to see him for themselves and put him to death.

David became an outlaw.

Let's return to the story of David and Michal. We can learn more about his outlaw days. Years pass and David became king of Judah. He established Jerusalem as his house, his favored city, built his army and set out to insure that Saul's descendants, whoever they may be, were not able to make a claim for the throne. Unfortunately, as we will read in a subsequent story, Saul's oldest and surviving son Ish-bosheth claimed the North. His uncle Abner became his general and schlepped Ish-bosheth from tribe to tribe to obtain their support. Unfortunately, he wasn't much of a leader and Abner eventually lost faith and sought to re-unite with David. (more about that later).

David threatened Ish-bosheth and demanded his sister, David's first wife Michal, be handed over to him and Ish-bosheth acquiesced.

Abner immediately sent messengers to David, saying, Make a pact with me, and I will help bring all Israel over to your side.

David replied, "Good but I make one demand, do not appear before me unless you bring Michal, daughter of Saul, when you come before me." David also sent messengers to Ish-bosheth demanding his wife Michal, for whom I paid the bride price of one hundred Philistine foreskins.

Ish-bosheth, acquiesced and had her taken from her husband Paltiel son of Laish.

Husband? She had a husband! Yes, apparently a husband who loved her because he followed her as far as Bahurim, weeping, until most likely, at the threat of death, he was forced to retreat.

Let's fast forward to Michal standing in her tower, looking at her husband. Her oh so loyal husband, the one who abandoned her, accumulated another five wives, stole her away from her family, from a man she dearly loved and who loved her, looking down at David.

What was she supposed to say to the man who ruined her life? What was she supposed to do with a husband who denied her his physical companionship because he wanted to assure that his predecessors' descendants never claimed his throne?

Oh Michal, poor Michal, I wish you had had better.

What can a modern learn from this story?

If you knew that Ish-bosheth meant "a shamed man", and that bahurim meant "boys", would that change or enhance your understanding of the story?

I realize that these people lived in less civilized times but it causes me to wonder if unintended pain and suffering can be avoided in one's drive to power.

THE INCIDENT OF RIZPAH, ISH-BOSHETH AND ABNER

Just prior to learning more about the future of Michal, our story diverges and we are told that Saul has died and David is hard at work solidifying his position. He is rightly concerned that one of Saul's descendants might challenge his bid for the throne.

The text informs us that prior to his death Saul had slaughtered many of the Gibeonites, a tribe that descended from the Amorites. Those who survived considered Saul anything but a friend.
Also prior to Saul's death, David was king of the breakaway kingdom of Judah. Saul's death resulted in David doing everything he could think of in order to consolidate his position so that he could eventually become king of a united kingdom.

David's primary rival was Ish-bosheth, Saul's son and legitimate heir. Initially, Saul's general Abner, also his nephew and a possible heir to the throne, believed Ish-bosheth could serve as king. Abner schlepped him throughout the Northern Kingdom in order to obtain the tribes' needed political support. At some point he realized that Ish-bosheth lacked the strength and character to rule. And, at some point which we are not told of, Abner slept with Saul's concubine Rizpah, daughter of Ish-bosheth (yes, Saul's own granddaughter was his concubine). After being admonished for fooling around with his liege's daughter and his father's mistress, Ish-bosheth verbally abused his Lord. Following this, Abner defects to David's camp.

Imagine how Ish-bosheth must have felt! It reads like a soap opera.

Let's return to David, now King David who was aggressively consolidating his power and was concerned that someone related to Saul could gather a force and challenge him. He recalled that the Gibeonites, at least what was left of them, were far from being Saul's supporters. He asked them what it would take to ally with him. They wished to be compensated the old fashioned way. An eye for an eye, or to simply state it, the death of seven of Saul's sons, the sons of Rizpah and the sons of Saul's oldest daughter, the one he was supposed to have married, Merab. Somehow, David, the man who would never harm the king, allied with the Gibeonites who, armed with the knowledge of the whereabouts of Rizpah's two sons and five of the sons of Merab…

> *The Gibeonites put them to death and hung up their bodies at the sanctuary at Gibeah.* (2 Samuel 21:8-9)

And then Rizpah took on the establishment.
> *She went to the rock of Gibeah and for five months guarded the suspended bodies of her children preventing their bodies from being devoured by beasts of prey and the birds of prey.* (2 Samuel 21:10)

Imagine,

> *…she took sackcloth and spread it on a rock and she stayed there from the beginning of the harvest until rain from the sky fell on the bodies. She did not let the birds of the sky settle on them by day or the wild beasts approach at night.*

There aren't a lot of roads traversing Israel today and there must have been even fewer three thousand years ago. Traders and soldiers and travelers passed by and saw this lonely woman dressed in mourning sitting on a rock protecting her dead decaying children's bodies.

Eventually, this became a national incident, one which forced David to move the bodies and bury them with dignity in their home town. There is more to this story (and it starts here).

THE STORY OF RIZPAH

Written by Micah, Grandson of Saul

THE STORY OF RIZPAH (2 SAMUEL 21)

My name is Micah. I am the great-grandson of Saul, first king of Israel. I live in David's court with my father Mephiposheth, who because of his physical disability, could never be considered a candidate for king. There is also a possibility that I am still alive because the old king was very close with my grandfather Jonathan. I'm not certain.
I maintain a low profile. I am athletic but don't excel. I wrestle and engage in gymnastics but never compete with a knife, spear of sword. I am not the court jester but at times act like one. There is nowhere else to go.

I have a lot of time to read. I recently read two versions of the same story. It was the story of one of my near distant relatives. We've never met. If she is still alive it would be too dangerous. She was the mistress of my great-grandfather Saul. They had two sons. I first read about her in last month's version of "The Jerusalem Gazette" because David had just arranged for the state burial of her two sons along with my grandfather and great-grandfather. It was a big deal.

David had traveled to Jabesh-Gilead and where he claimed the remains of Saul and Jonathan, who had been taken by the Philistines and hung in the square at Beth Shean after the battle of Mt. Gilboa. He'd had the bodies transported to their ancestral home in Benjamin and where they were buried.

The "Benjamina", a monthly which is published in Beth El and serves the population of Dan, Ephraim and of course, Benjamin, suggested a different spin. I'm not certain if that newspaper will survive. I love the way they write.

This is what they reported.

Immediately following Saul's death, Abner, Saul's former general, took my great-uncle Ish-bosheth, and schlepped him from town to town, village to village, and tribe to tribe proclaiming him to be Saul's successor. Everyone was frightened. Saul had just been defeated by the Philistines who were reaching out to each of their five cities seeking additional soldiers. Things weren't looking good - they were claiming this was their opportunity to send us back to Egypt.

Samuel had died, and the only other possible leader was that southerner, that brigand, David. Excuse me, for what I just said. It slipped out. Don't let it leave the room. They really didn't have a choice - they accepted him to be their king.

David had already threatened Ish-bosheth and demanded the return of his first wife, my great-aunt, Michal. Ish-bosheth acquiesced. He literally packed her bags and sent her packing. I heard it was a painful experience and her husband followed her as far as Abner permitted, crying all the way.

My investigations have led me to believe that by releasing his sister, my great-aunt, and sending her to David, he literally relinquished his right to the throne.

My great-uncle must have disappointed Abner because just before Abner abandoned him and transferred his allegiance to David, he slept with Saul's mistress. How embarrassing. She must have been extremely attractive or Abner was toying with making himself king. Oh by the way, her name was Rizpah.

My great-uncle Ish-bosheth confronted Abner, who responded in a threatening tone that who he slept with was none of his business. Ish-bosheth was intimidated and remained silent. Shortly after this incident Abner transferred his loyalty to David. Ish-bosheth reigned for two years. He didn't die in his sleep.

Sometime later, Absalom rebelled. David almost lost the kingdom. He wasn't as young as he used to be and his judgment and confidence often wavered. He feared additional rebellions would occur and so he sought to learn if any of Saul's descendants were still alive.

"The Jerusalem Gazette" claims his subsequent actions were motivated by a famine that was taking place. They said he inquired of the Lord who explained the famine was a result of the blood guilt committed by the late King Saul. Really?

The spin from "The Royal Press" claimed Saul had violated an oath he had made to his onetime allies, the Amorites. In return for their allegiance they were promised the right to coexist in his kingdom. Saul, in a moment of zeal, attempted to wipe them out leaving the Gibeonites as the only remnant of the Amorite people.

David, according to "The Gazette" attempted to make amends and summoned the Gibeonites to his court. He asked what could be done to rectify this grievous error. Bottom line: they didn't want silver or gold but they would be satisfied if seven men, the last descendants of Saul, were handed over to them to be impaled.

And David, honorable David, agreed.

Armoni and Mephibosheth, the two sons of Rizpah, and the five sons of Merab (another of my great-aunts), were hung from their hands with spears in their guts. And of course as a result of this righteous deed, the rains returned, the crops began to grow. The Lord responded to the land's plea.

"The Benjamini" saw right through this political ruse and most likely would have been shut down if noble Rizpah's actions hadn't become a matter of national concern.

She went to the crossroads where her children had been hung and cut them down. And then she stripped off her clothing and replaced it with sackcloth. She covered herself with ashes and sat on a rock and stayed there from the beginning of the harvest and until the rains fell. She sat on a rock for an entire season and did not let the birds of the sky settle on her loved ones and pick their bones by day or the wild beasts approach by night to feast upon their remains. She sat for an entire season. And she grieved.
There aren't many roads in our country and Rizpah sat at a major intersection. Within a few days everyone, and I mean everyone, traders, cara-

vans, farmers, soldiers, who walked on that road saw a woman dressed in sackcloth grieving over and protecting corpses from wild beasts. She stood guard over those bodies, those decaying putrefying corpses that was all that was left of her children day and night during the long hot summer.

> *"I have made the crags my home, and spread*
> *On their desert backs my sackcloth bed;*
> *I have eaten the bitter herb of the rocks,*
> *And drunk the midnight dew in my locks;*
> *And driven the vulture and raven away*
> *I have wept till I could not weep, and the pain*
> *Of my burning eyeballs went to my brain.*
> *Seven blackened corpses before me lie,*
> *In the blaze of the sun and the winds of the sky,*
> *I have watched them through the burning day,*
> *I have watched them through the burning day,*
> *And driven the vulture and raven away;*
> *And the cormorant wheeled in circles around,*
> *yet feared to alight on the guarded ground.*
> *And when the shadows of twilight came,*
> *I have seen hyena's eyes of flame.*
> *And heard at my side his stealthy tread.*
> *But aye, at my shout the savage fled;*
> *And I threw the lighted brand to fright*
> *The jackal and wolf that yelled in the night.*
> *Ye were foully murdered, my hapless sons,*
> *By the hands of the wicked and cruel ones;*
> *Ye fell, in your fresh and blooming prime,*
> *All innocent, for your father's crime."* [2]

And eventually, eventually, word of Rizpah's noble act trickled up to Jerusalem. People began to wonder what or who was responsible for this tragedy. And the longer Rizpah remained the greater the embarrassment no, the threat to the administration became. Finally, it couldn't be ignored and David was forced to take action.

[2] Excerpted from Rizpah, William Cullen Bryant 1794-1878

I have to admit he did it with style. He exhumed the bones of Saul, and Jonathan, gathered the bones of the impaled sons of Rizpah and Merab, and transported them in honor to their ancestral home. He had buried them with dignity in the territory of Benjamin in the tomb of Saul's father, Kish. One thing about David, he did things in style.

In my eyes, Rizpah was the strongest woman in the Bible. Her courage and her moral strength and indignation forced a government to action. There is so much we can learn from her.

Sometimes it takes pain to make a hero. Sometimes it is the need to stand up and speak or act against oppression.

Like David standing against Goliath, Rizpah challenged the establishment.

And sometimes so must we.

MY UNCLE, MY LEIGE

Written by Joab, Nephew of David
(1 Kings 2:29-34)

I t's only a matter of time. An hour perhaps two before Beniah returns. I don't have much time left. I was wise to make my stand to position my-self in the Tent of the Lord. It would make him hesitate and it will serve as a testimony to my loyalty to the Kingdom and my integrity to those who wish to remember. I don't care what the king requested, I won't fall on my sword. If they want me dead and they do, they will have to kill me.

My name is Joab. It's somewhat ironic that I, a nephew of David, former twice captain of his armies, a man loyal to the current and future nation, a man who assisted him every step of the way in his rise to power, a man who helped him pacify, unite and expand the land and the nation, should be killed by his successor as a last wish of my former liege. Beniah, my disciple will have to do it if he wishes to remain Captain of the Host.

I have so little remaining time, yet if I think back and consider if I could do it all again, would I have behaved differently? I think not. I think the friendship and the rivalry that existed between me and my uncle, my king, was inevitable. We are, well we were, men with strong emotional commit-ments to those we loved and to the ideals to which we adhered. He knew he was meant to build a nation, and I understood my role to further his interests in building a strong united kingdom.
The trouble began with the death of my brother Abishai. It was the first of four incidents that ultimately led to my imminent demise.

The first one occurred on the eve of the civil war.

Saul and his son Jonathan had been killed by the Philistines at Gilboa; Ish-bosheth, Saul's remaining son, could have and should have inherited the crown. Abner, Saul's general, had taken charge. He paraded Ish-bosheth to all of the northern tribes and proclaimed him king. It certainly made sense.

The kingdom required a leader to defend against the Philistines and David had been outlawed by Saul. But Ish-bosheth was so, so weak and ineffective. First he capitulated to David and gave him back his sister, David's former wife, Michal. Oh, was that painful! Ish-bosheth commanded Abner to forcibly separate her from her husband and loved ones. It was just a matter of time before he became so disgusted with him that he slept with Rizpah, Saul's former concubine, and further embarrassed and demeaned Ish-bosheth (Rizpah's father).

The North stood loyal to Ish-bosheth, and the South sided with the only person who commanded men, David. I remember when we went to the pool of Gibeon, Abner and I, each with a dozen soldiers. It started as a jest, a little sport but it developed into much more than a military exercise. At first it seemed like fun, a friendly competition but loyalties ran high, tempers escalated and soldiers began to die. Abner and his entourage were decisively beaten.

My younger brother Asahel was with us and was caught in the moment. He pursued Abner and Abner, in deference to him, did not wish to kill him and pleaded with him to desist and return to my camp. But he was young and hot blooded and inexperienced and he refused. Abner tried three times and finally, in the hopes of preventing his death, turned aside and attempted to stun him with a backward thrust. It failed, he died.

Abner killed my youngest brother.
Shortly afterwards Abner abandoned Ish-bosheth He needed to follow a strong leader and could no longer tolerate an incompetent one. He transferred his allegiance to David strengthening David's position amongst the northern tribes. My brother was still dead and I had acquired a rival.

For some reason, David held me responsible for my brother's death and refused to chastise Abner. David's brother Abishai and I both knew revenge was required. It was the honorable thing to do. Perhaps David was hesitant because Abner's death could shatter the fragile alliance between North and

South. But my brother's death cried out to be avenged.

I wish I had the courage to overcome my instincts that I learned to control later on when David placed me in what could only be described as the most uncomfortable situation in my life, but at that moment I couldn't, I just couldn't let go of it. He was so young and full of life and at the moment when David could unite the country, I committed an act of political stupidity. I killed Abner.

David cursed me. He publicly humiliated me. He made me rend my clothes and gird myself with sackcloth and mourn Abner. He removed me from office. But he allowed me to remain alive. Perhaps it was because he lacked the political strength. Perhaps it was because he knew the army and the people were sympathetic. "I am this day weak, a just anointed king; and the sons of Zeruiah are too hard for me."

In order to insure his innocence David composed a dirge and proclaimed a day of fasting.

"So all the people and all Israel understood that day that it was not of the king to slay Abner".

In his early days he was a great politician. It took my leading a major military initiative against the Jebusites for me to be reappointed Captain of the Host.

The second incident that seriously altered our relationship was when he became involved with Uriah's wife, Bathsheba.

David loved women. He had many wives and at least an equal number of concubines and that didn't include the occasional roadside dalliance if you know what I mean. I'm not being judgmental. It was more or less what men with power did in those days. But he made a big mistake when he messed with Bathsheba.

She wasn't just another attractive woman. She was Uriah's wife. Uriah, a man who had fought and drank and partied with him for more than twenty years. Uriah, who began to serve him before he became king. Uriah, one of David's valiant men.
He could have had any woman but he had to attach himself to the wife of someone he had known for nearly twenty years. And then he had the nerve

to have me send him to the front lines where the fighting was the thickest. I basically arranged for Uriah's death so David could have a little cooch.

I loved Uriah, but I loved my liege and my country more. I did what my king commanded and it burned.

I guess that's when he stopped being able to look me in the eye.

The third incident involves Absalom.

From that point onward, I continued to follow David's orders, and did what I was told, but the distance between us never lessened. I was careful not to eclipse him and I deferred to him in all matters. The country was united, David was in his early fifties and a successor had not been appointed. Everyone thought it would be Amnon, his first born, but he after Amnon seduced and raped his half-sister Tamar, and then publicly humiliated her, he fell from favor. All of us were surprised he was never punished. It was obvious that he deeply regretted his act - but not to be punished?

Tamar's brother, Absalom, witnessed her pain and her shame. He found her screaming and covered with ashes in the street. He didn't forget. Two years later Absalom arranged for Amnon to be murdered and immediately afterwards fled to his grandfather's home where he remained for three years until I contrived to bring him back to comfort his loving father. I remember David mourned for Amnon but he grieved for Absalom.

My king was in mourning and the country was in need. In desperation I arranged a little charade that forced David to stop grieving and to request Absalom's return. David was so smart, he saw right through my effort and asked the woman from Tekoah if I was responsible for her tale. She acknowledged the truth:

"Yes, your servant Joab was the one who instructed me, and it was he, who told me everything to say."

Then the king said to Joab: "I will do this thing. Go and bring back my boy Absalom."

Absalom was just like his father, charismatic, charming and ambitious.

No one in all Israel was so admired for his beauty as Absalom; from the sole of his foot to the crown of his head he was without blemish. When he cut his hair - he had to have it cut every year, for it grew too heavy for him - the hair of his head weighed two hundred shekels by the royal weight. He had three sons and a daughter named Tamar.

Within two years of his return he was plotting rebellion. He travelled throughout the country extending hand to be kissed and claiming if he had the authority he would right all wrongs. He plotted and politicked for forty years and after he sent messengers to all the tribes and invited them to join him in Hebron where he was going to offer sacrifice.

Absalom commanded the army and David, my king, was forced to flee for his life. Saul's son Mephiboshet hoped the kingdom would be returned to him, Shimea the son of Gera, a member of Saul's clan, threw stones at him and screamed insults. And as David fled, Absalom entered Jerusalem. In order to secure the thrown, Absalom lay with his father's concubines with the full knowledge of all Israel.

Absalom had two counselors: Ahithopel who advised him to take twelve thousand men and hunt the king down, and Hushai, a friend who suggested Absalom mobilize the entire country into a manhunt and find and kill David wherever he was hiding. David had loyal supporters who were in Absalom's camp. They advised him to gather his men and cross the Jordan. Once across the Jordan, David divided his troops into three commands, I took one, my brother Abishai led another and David's friend Ittai from Gath took the third.

David's troops confronted the Israelites, and as we left to do battle, he cautioned us to be kind to his son. My God what were we supposed to do? Kill the troops and save the culprit? I referred to Absalom's troops as Israelites because they were mostly composed of the northern tribes who still resented what David's usurpation of Saul's crown. The country might have been united but not firmly so. The battle took place. We were victorious!

It was a great slaughter, some say twenty-thousand men died. Absalom fled on a mule and as the mule ran under a tree, his hair- his beautiful hair- got caught in its branches and he was held between heaven and earth as the mule under him kept going.

Did I really have a choice? Should I have adhered to the wishes of my king and dared to lose a nation? Three quick darts finished it as he dangled before me in the tree. What else could I have done? Should I have saved him so he could plot another rebellion?

And David must have reasoned, first Abner and then my beloved son Absalom, Joab is out to get me. David mourned and went into a deep depression and the people began to wonder what was wrong with their king. They were ashamed and began to leave him.

I knew I was hated and my days on this earth were numbered but the nation needed a strong king and I, only I, had the credibility to wake him up. I rebuked David with sharp words.

"Why do you love those who hate you and hate those who loved you? You have a country that needs you, you're a king! Start acting like one!"

David was furious with me, He removed me from office a second time, but that time he had gone too far.

When Sheba ben Birchi led yet another revolt, David appointed a new commander Amasa to put it down. Amasa was inexperienced and would have lost the day or suffered tremendous losses. I pursued him and took over and ended the revolt with a minimum of bloodshed. The kingdom was reunited, and David retained his throne. A successor had yet to be appointed and I knew my days were numbered.

I must have but a few hours left. Benaih should have reached Solomon by this time and I know that he will be commanded to return and take my life. When this is ended I hope that it will be known that I truly gave my life for my country. It was out of my loyalty to my country that I committed treason.

David was sleeping with Bathsheba. Their first child had been born dead. David believed God was punishing him for his indiscretion. What? Just one little indiscretion? David's wife Bathsheba and his court prophet Nathan were plotting to get their second child, Solomon, proclaimed as king. Solomon was approaching his twentieth year when Adonijah, David's next eldest made his bid for the throne. David was so old and sick that at the age of seventy he had to grant audiences from his bed chamber. The kingdom was floundering. I made my final choice and this was the fourth incident which resulted in my doom.

I had always like Adonijah. He was charismatic, strong and understood the need for war. It's true I favored him over Solomon. Every time I looked at Solomon I saw my dead friend Uriah's face. I don't know what caused me to do it. I didn't have the support of the army, I was out of favor with the king but on some level I believed that he would best serve the country. He would unite the factions, defend us from invaders and make us whole again once more.

As David was dying he instructed Solomon ... "You know what Joab, son of Zeruiah did unto me, and what he did to Abner and unto Absalom and Amasa. Do according to your wisdom and let not his grey head go down in peace."

The tent is very warm, I am glad I chose to end my life in this special place. It is the place where oaths are taken and loyalties are upheld. I can see the shadow of Beniah grasping his sword as he enters the tent. I remember my uncle telling me the story of the time God spoke to him just prior to the battle with Goliath.

In spite of everything he pledged himself to God. And God, I suppose, loved him and forgave him because that's what the true God does. His pledge was to God, mine was to a nation which I hope will survive. Perhaps if we had been better men we could have done it better. I just hope, hello Beniah, I am ready, that in the future both of us were correct.

SOLOMON'S AMAZING

TECHNICOLOR PRESS AGENT

There are two ways to view the stories of David and Solomon. The first way is how the text actually reads. Taken literally, the stories reflect a world when epics were created. This view was shaped by the theology of a later time, and as such could limit our ability to connect with the text and to realize its full importance. There are some who suggest we should understand these stories as partial memories of our ancient past. Memories which have been magnified over time and that morphed into legends rather than reflect what actually occurred.

The first way portrays David as an honorable leader, a dynamic general who had a vision to create a united kingdom of Israel governed from a holy place. Solomon is similarly depicted as a wise, able almost magically gifted leader. The builder of the Temple was like his father, one who was loved by God.

But both of these characters have a darker, weaker side. David's failure to address succession coupled with an extremely active libido, were ultimately responsible for his tragic later years. Solomon eventually soils his reputation as the builder of the Temple and man of great wisdom, and succumbs to the lure of foreign women and their gods. His vast harem of Moabite, Amnonite, Edomite, Sidonian, and Hittite wives introduced pagan worship into the holy city. As a result, the text tells us, God became angry and fostered a series of rebellions by once conquered peoples. These revolts weakened Solomon's kingdom and following his death, the ten northern tribes seceded from the union and established a separate kingdom.

The division of the kingdom caused the authors of our text difficulty because God had given an eternal, unconditional promise that David's throne would be established forever (2 Samuel 7:16), and the Davidic dynasty would never fade away. The final authors of our text shaped the text and specifically the stories of David and Solomon with a specific intent. They placed great emphasis on their roles in centralizing Jerusalem as the central place of worship and holiness. But this didn't begin with David and Solomon; it actually began several hundred years later. The second way of viewing these texts is by removing the theological implications and replacing them with what historical and archeological research has determined. One of the benefits of this method is that the reader can gain an understanding of how literature in the ancient world developed and how the characters in those stories become more real, more human.

So let's first examine what the Bible tells us and after that review it with a possible historical overlay.

WHO WAS SOLOMON?

Solomon, the second son of David and Bathsheba, was the third king of Israel. He reigned from about 971 B.C.E. to 931 B.C.E. Their first son died in childbirth supposedly as a punishment for David's sending Bathsheba's first husband and David's friend, Uriah, to his death. Nathan the court prophet originally named Solomon "Jedidiah", meaning the beloved of YHWH, but it was changed, most likely by his press agent to Solomon. Solomon can be translated to mean "peaceful". Bathsheba was most likely a politically astute mother, who guided him in his early years and was most likely partially responsible for the reputation he developed; after all she managed to have him recognized as the next king while David was on his deathbed.

The prophetic passage that is found in 1 Kings 1 (the haftarah for the portion Hayyei Sarah) sheds light on the intrigue surrounding the Solomon's selection as David's successor. Unlike in the books of Chronicles where Solomon is easily and divinely proclaimed, this version describes the transition from father to son as a coup, perpetuated by Solomon's mother Bathsheba and the court prophet Nathan. David, at this point was weak, old and possibly impotent. There are some who claim that having a young beautiful virgin lie on top of him to keep him warm was a sign of his impotence. Others of course understood this as a guy thing and as a challenge to see if he could rise to the occasion.

As David was approaching the end of his life, his next eldest son, Adonijah, (1 Kings 1) attempted to claim the throne. The text informs us that he failed to send invitations to his coronation, to some of the David's most influential friends and advisers, as well as his younger half-brother Solomon. This aroused the suspicion of Nathan, David's prophet, who arranged for David to formally acknowledge Solomon as his successor and King of Israel, at the same time that Adonijah was being crowned. Somehow with a young beautiful girl lying on top of him, his most recent wife and her advisors managed to obtain his agreement for their twelve-year-old son to become king. Good work!

Imagine a pre-bar mitzvah adolescent becoming king of a nation and having to immediately contend with his successful, more qualified older brother. And this is where our story begins. As soon as Adonijah learned of Solomon's coronation, he fled and claimed sanctuary at the altar, and would only leave that holy place if Solomon swore to spare his life.
The text of 1 Kings 2: 1-12 (the haftarah corresponding to the Torah portion for Va-yechi) describes David's last moments and his charge to Solomon. While apparently extremely frail his mind is still intact. He advises his son what needs to be accomplished if he wishes to retain his kingdom. And Solomon follows his advice, or perhaps both of his parents' advice. He immediately consolidates his position and removes or arranges to have any possible threats to his office removed.

THE FIRST REBELLION

One of David's most serious flaws, one which plagued him his entire life, was his failure to appoint a successor. The first time this caused a problem was when his favorite son, Absalom, attempted a coup. Absalom, the first son, defended his half-sister Tamar after his half-brothers, Amnon, raped her. He must have been very close with Tamar, because he waited for two years and then he took his revenge and arranged for Amnon's death. Some things just can't be covered up. Absalom fled into exile leaving a father grieving. The text is unclear whether David grieved for his dead son or because his most beloved son had fled.

And David rent his garment and lay down on the ground.

It took all of Joab's (David's advisor) diplomatic skill to bring father and son together. It's an interesting story; the relationship was ruptured, never to be completely healed. Over the next several years Absalom prepared his rebellion. He aggressively developed popular support. He sent messengers to the tribes inviting them to his coronation. He gathered an army and he administered justice. In other words, he attempted to function as a king. We are told that after forty years Absalom went to Hebron, an older city still harboring people who were not fully supportive of David's move to Jerusalem and had himself proclaimed king. Forty years is the Bible's way of telling us "a long time."

And he created an army and marched on Jerusalem. When word of this came to David he was forced to leave his palace and flee.

So the King left, followed by his entire household, except for ten concubines whom the king left to mind the palace.

And the whole countryside wept aloud as the troops marched by. The king crossed the valley of Kidron.

David was completely unprepared. He was forced to flee and hide in the wilderness and forced to rely on food donations to survive. David had passed a little beyond the summit of Mount Olives when a servant of Mephibosheth came with a pair of saddled asses carrying two hundred loaves of bread and wine and cakes for him and his household. Mephibosheth was the last of Saul's grandsons and because of an infirmity could never serve as King. David responded to this gift derisively.

Do you think that your family will once again rule?

As David fled from Jerusalem, Absalom entered it. At this point the text becomes really interesting (2 Samuel 16-19). Absalom is convinced by Aphipotel, let's call him his advisor, to sleep with David's concubines in order to demonstrate his mastery of the kingdom. He further advises him to send an army of twelve thousand men, probably one thousand from each tribe, to attack David and kill him while he is weary and weak of heart.

As a result of all the intrigue, David regains his throne and Absalom, handsome Absalom who was known for his long beautiful hair, flees riding a mule. As the mule passes under a great terebinth tree his hair became tangled within it its briars leaving him stuck "between heaven and earth."

Joab, David's nephew and military commander, finished the job. David never forgave him:

> *Is my boy safe? Is my boy safe? He went up to the upper chamber and wept. Moaning these words as he went, "My son, Absalom! O my son, my son Absalom! If only I had died instead of you! O Absalom, my son, my son.* (2 Samuel 18:9)

David might have been a brilliant general and a forceful leader but the relationships he had with his children left much to be desired.

I like to think of him as a man who might have heard and listened to God's voice when he was young. But over time, as he became more successful and life became more politically complicated, he lost that vision and that voice and succumbed to the pressures of the world. He favored one child over the others and was a failure at family and succession planning. To his credit, he was the first leader of his time to employ a chronicler. A chronicler? That sounds like a modern press agent.

One can learn a lot about what not to do and how not to be a leader in a family from studying the life of David, the man whom God loved the most. His failure to plan was consistent with his poor parenting skills.

Solomon could have learned a lot from his father. His father loved the women and had many wives. Solomon had more. His father knew how to maintain his authority at any cost. Solomon, as we will learn later on, had similar skills. David failed to train a successor, Solomon followed in his father's footsteps. Finally, David had great political acumen. He was the first king to employ a chronicler, one who wrote or rewrote history in his favor. What David did, Solomon did ten times better.

Now let's view this story through an historical/archeological lens.

The text assumes that David lived in the tenth century B.C.E. This roughly placed Saul, his predecessor, at the beginning of the first Iron Age. At that time, according to archeologists, Jerusalem was a small, sparsely inhabited village surrounded by a few pastoral permanent settlements. Prior to David's conquest of Jerusalem, actually during his bandit days, a letter to the Egyptian Pharaoh from the ruler of Jerusalem requesting military aid against the many bands of outlaws was received. This could have been from the historical David. During this period the majority of the population lived in the north which was on the major trade routes. A century later, Jerusalem (in the south) became the city of David and a series of administrative centers were established in Lachish, Beth Shemesh, Beersheva and Arad.

According to Israel Finkelstein and Neil Silberman in their work *The Bible Unearthed : Archaeology's New Vision of Ancient Israel and the Origin of Its Sacred Texts,* by the eighth century B.C.E. (700s) the Northern Kingdom had been conquered by the Assyrians and Judah (Jerusalem) had become an Assyrian vassal. This was the period of the building of the Siloam tunnel and King Hezekiah. This was a time of significant population growth in Jerusalem, most likely because of the refugees who fled from the north, and the growth of the olive oil and scribal industries. It was at this time that ballads about both David and Solomon were most likely written. But it still wasn't the time when the authors of these stories linked David and his descendants to the concept of Messiah. The Hebrew word *mashiach* actually means anointed one even though most people today assume it means Messiah. It wasn't until 609 B.C.E that the word *mashiach,* nearly four hundred years after David's death, became linked to the Davidic dynasty.

It happened when the then King, Josiah, was killed at Megiddo. Judaism and Christianity have never forgotten Megiddo. Josiah was killed by the Pharaoh, Neco, while defending his Babylonian masters and his servants carried him from Megiddo to be buried in Jerusalem.

A few centuries later, the word was translated in Greek and the term, "Armageddon" was born. Megiddo is still recalled as the fateful spot where the forces of good and evil would someday do battle and determine the fate of the world. At that time, a righteous king of Davidic lineage would return to where the last righteous Davidic king had perished.

SOLOMON: THE EARLY YEARS

Our text informs us that Solomon, a twelve or thirteen-year old boy, immediately took charge of his life upon becoming king. This wasn't easy because his father had left him with many dangling modifiers.

First he had to deal with his elder brother Adonijah, his immediate rival. Adonijah, through Bathsheba, the queen-mother, asked the king for permission to marry Abishag the Shunammite. This request was equivalent to asking to be a co-regent. Solomon responded quickly. He sent Benaiah to slay him.

Solomon needed to address all of the conspirators quickly. His next command addressed the problem of Abiathar, David's trusted priest, the one who had conspired with Adonijah. He was sent to the priestly-city Anathoth, and deprived of his priestly office. Joab, the third member of the troika upon learning of Adonijah's fate, fled to the altar for refuge. Solomon quickly took care of him.

Finally, Shimei, the man who had cursed David and was suspected of inciting a rebellion was given explicit orders to remain in Jerusalem where his movements would be known. Unfortunately, when two of his servants escaped to Philistia he left Jerusalem in order to capture them. He was placed upon Beniah's list and upon his return was similarly taken care of. These initial actions resolved any immediate threat to Solomon's life. The throne was now secure.

Let's take a look at how he ruled.
Having achieved temporary security, Solomon married Pharaoh's daughter and established Egypt as an ally. 1 Kings provides us with situations that exemplify his wisdom and greatness of character all leading up to his decision to construct the Temple.

Solomon, like his father, can be viewed through two lenses: the first is how he was portrayed in the Bible and the second is how he is portrayed in legend. The second wonders about the reality of his life.

According to the text, Solomon's administration was more sophisticated than his father's. He created twelve prefects, most likely to correspond to each of the tribes even though the areas attributed to the prefects didn't exactly correspond to the tribal boundaries. This blending of property that overlapped tribal boundaries most likely was intended to weaken tribal authority and strengthen the centrality of Jerusalem.

The book of Kings describes him as one who amassed great wealth. This in part was due to the claim that he received tribute from two territories ruled by a tribe called Palastu or Philistia. The prefects were responsible for provisioning the royal household (taxes), and maintaining horsemen and chariots (an army). Actually, this level of sophistication was probably not the case but the authors of the text clearly wished Solomon to be viewed as a brilliant administrator, an excellent business person, and someone who excelled in wisdom.

Perhaps he learned the art of self-promotion from his father because his legend has reached across time and faiths.

The Koran depicts him as a man of great wisdom, knowledge, and power. According to their scripture, he knew the "language of the birds" and was known in the Islam to have other supernatural abilities (bestowed upon him by God after a special request by Solomon himself) The Koran explains he had the power to control the wind, that he ruled over the Jinn and demons. The Islamic tradition attributes to Solomon the saying: "The beginning of wisdom is the fear of God".

Solomon even found his way into the *One Thousand and One Nights.*

A well-known story in the collection *One Thousand and One Nights* describes a genie that had displeased King Solomon and was punished by being locked in a bottle and thrown into the sea. Since the bottle was sealed with Solomon's seal, the genie was helpless to free itself, until freed many centuries later by a fisherman who discovered the bottle. In other stories found in *One Thousand and One Nights,* protagonists who had to leave their homeland and travel to the unknown places of the world saw signs that proved that Solomon had already been there. Sometimes, protagonists discovered Solomon's words which aimed to help those who were lost and unluckily reached those forbidden and deserted places.

In the Bahá'í faith, Solomon is regarded as one of the lesser prophets along with David, Isaiah, Jeremiah, Ezekiel and others.

And in our rabbinic tradition, angels helped Solomon build the Temple. The Temple, according to rabbinic legend, was miraculously constructed of large heavy stones rising and settling in their respective places. The general opinion of the Talmudic rabbis was that Solomon hewed the stones by means of a *shamir,* a mythical worm whose mere touch cleft rocks. According to *Midrash Tehillim,* the shamir was brought from paradise by Solomon's eagle. But most of the rabbis disagreed and explained that Solomon was informed of the worm's abilities by Asmodeus. The *shamir* had been entrusted by the prince of the sea to the mountain rooster alone, and the rooster had sworn to guard it well, but Solomon's men found the bird's nest, and covered it with glass. When the bird returned, it used the *shamir* to break the glass, whereupon the men scared the bird, causing it to drop the worm, which the men could then bring to Solomon.

Early adherents of the *Kabbalah* (Jewish mystical tradition) portrayed Solomon as having sailed through the air on a throne of light placed on an eagle, which brought him near the heavenly gates as well as to the dark mountains behind which the fallen angels Uzza and Azzazel were chained; the eagle would rest on the chains, and Solomon, using the magic ring, would compel the two angels to reveal every mystery he desired to know.

Suffice it to say that by the seventh century B.C.E. Solomon was described as wise, an extremely successful builder, and a brilliant merchant who sent expeditions to foreign lands. All of this is comparable to what can be described as high Assyrian style. This was the time of Assyrian domination, when King Manasseh, a man whom the Bible describes as the most despised king in the Bible, ruled Judah as a satrap. The authors of our text chose not to inform us that under Manasseh's rule, Judah experienced its longest and most economically prosperous period since the kingdoms separated after the death of Solomon.

Historians and archeologists verify that the stories about Solomon reflect an accurate history memory of someone else. The vision of a large united kingdom had nothing to do with the version in 1 Kings 4:26-28 because at that time Jerusalem was composed of a series of poor villages with limited agricultural abilities. This was the time of King Manasseh, (698-642 B.C.E.) a brilliant king who in spite of having to pay a huge tribe to Assyria was able to maximize Judah's agricultural potential.

It was during Manasseh's time that the queen of Sheba in distant Yemen came to visit. Sheba was famous for its caravans of camels. It was during Manasseh's time that the province of Judah became famous for its breeding of the highly prized Ethiopian horses. We actually don't know who built the First Temple in Jerusalem. Perhaps it was Solomon but certainly on a lesser scale.

The epics of David and Solomon, wonderful stories about heroes of long past, optimize the amazing wondrous process that became our Bible. Like our patriarchs and matriarchs, they provide us with anecdotes about real people with great strengths and similar weaknesses. Like the patriarchs and matriarchs they challenge us by studying what has been recorded as portions of their lives to wrestle with the choices we have to make and as a result, hopefully inspire us to become better human beings.

Many of us have a tendency to idolize famous people. It doesn't matter if they are politicians, actors or athletes. We place them on a pedestal. However, if we peel the legend away from the actual person a different picture emerges. The David and Solomon of legend lift our spirits and possibly, hopefully, encourage us to dream. This is a good thing. Perhaps legendary stories provide us with the strength and courage to step out of the normality of life and make a difference. At the same time the actual lives of David and Solomon and everyone else, help us to understand that all of us are mortal. We make mistakes and most often do the best we can.

Perhaps we need to synthesize these two ways of understanding. Give it some thought.

Section 3

RESPONDING TO UNANSWERED QUESTIONS
Some Theories and Some History

INTRODUCTION

Following the destruction of the Second Temple the rabbis emerged as the new royalty and as far as we can tell were responsible for the shaping of religious life. How this actually occurred remains a mystery as a result of the limited sources and knowledge that are currently available. Thankfully, scholars in a numerous related fields continue to discover new information which often results in existent theories being discarded and replaced by more current ones.

Unfortunately, a great deal of the material being written which sheds additional light on the development of Judaism is rarely widely disseminated. This results in a huge knowledge and time gap between those who could transmit this newly acquired knowledge and those who have discovered it. This is one of three reasons why I have written this book and its predecessor, *Biblical Leadership After Moses: Lessons to be Learned.*

The second reason is a combination of my need to better understand the text so I could it teach it in a way that resonated with people, and also deepened their appreciation in order to answer some of their most basic questions. Questions which I have heard over and over from people who just want to know "why". The final reason is because I'm something of a plodder. I need to write about a topic before I feel comfortable enough to teach it.

The essays that follow attempt provide answers to those questions that one continuously hears and are almost always left unanswered. For the most part they are my theories based upon what I have learned from those who really do the research.

Finally, the essay devoted to the Samaritan was written out of frustration. I can't tell you how many times, well-meaning Christians called me "A Good Samaritan" after observing me perform some simple act of lovingkindness. I am not a Good Samaritan, and while I assume there are Samaritans who are good people, none of them should be equated with the Good Samaritan mentioned in Christian scripture.

ATTEMPTING TO EXPLAIN JUDAISM'S SURVIVAL

A Trip Back in Time to Babylon

Until just a few decades ago, archeological research in the Middle East was almost solely focused on justifying the veracity of the incidents and places referred to in the Bible. Once historians and archeologists were able to confirm or reject those assumptions, the vision of what actually took place during Biblical times changed drastically. This new way of understanding the Bible can provide us with needed information that can strengthen our connections to Israel and to the values being promoted within our religious traditions.

How may we explain the reasons for Judaism's survival? Perhaps a good starting point would be assuming that the seeds of the Jewish continuity puzzle are rooted in the time shortly before and during the period of the Babylonian exile, and that this period should be viewed through the lens of the exilic community and how it adapted to the larger more sophisticated Babylonian culture.

In the past two thousand years, we have rarely taken into account the importance and the influence that occurred in Babylon. Yet the theological and political concepts that governed Babylonian society were responsible for shaping Second Temple life and what eventually several hundred years later, became the rabbinic tradition. For better or for worse, the texts which we consider to be the holiest object in our tradition have been overshadowed for two thousand years by their successor, the Talmud. We don't learn *Tanach* for its own sake. In the realm of the *yeshiva,* students learned Bible almost solely from providing proof texts for Talmudic interpretations of law and legends, a process that continues in some traditional parts of the Jewish world today. But even when people study Bible in the rest of the Jewish world, we usually do so without a proper understanding of the forces which shaped the texts.

The Torah, the five books of Moses, is our holiest text. The books that follow, the Prophets and Writings, also have canonical status which the Talmud does not. Furthermore, the stories in the books of Joshua, Judges, Prophets and Kings offer insight into a developing national historical religious tradition which has been shaped and edited as a result of centuries of international politics.

Finally, and perhaps most importantly, Western civilization has taught that basic values and religious teaching have their sources in the Bible. This disparity causes one to wonder what happened that lead to our under-emphasis of Bible study.

Most synagogue-attending Jews don't realize that a significant number of the prophetic portions *(haftarot)* which are chanted on Shabbat and holidays were not composed in Israel. We also don't realize that two items, the Torah and the Sabbath, the two anchors that are primarily responsible for the continuity of Jewish life, had their origins in Babylon.

What would Judaism look like with the Sabbath? Without the Torah? Without Torah study?

What we define as modern Judaism originated as result of the Babylonian exilic experience. When we research Babylonian religious practices we are able to discern parallels as well as points of departure, interesting points of departure, between the two cultures.

When one revisits the prophetic portions found in the *haftarot* from the books of Haggai, Zechariah, Malachi, Second Isaiah and Ezekiel and compared their visions and their messages with Babylonian religious practices and politics of the times, once can develop an understanding of what Judaism and Jewish life might have looked like before it became the form of Judaism based upon the Judaism that developed in Jerusalem.

The influence of Babylon itself, not the Jewish experience there, is not often taught in congregations, rarely mentioned from the pulpit, and most likely hardly ever included in adult education courses. Yet the theological and political concepts that governed Babylonian society were responsible for shaping Second Temple life and what eventually became, several hundred years later, rabbinic Judaism.

In order to understand the impact and importance of the Babylonian experience it is necessary to briefly summarize the religion of Israel during the First Temple period and to highlight the ideas and messages of the prophets who lived just prior to the exile and First Temple's destruction until the return to the land in 539 B.C.E.

WHAT DID WORSHIP/RELIGION LOOK LIKE DURING THE TIME OF THE FIRST TEMPLE?

Worship and belief in God or gods clearly existed in pre-Temple times but formal Temple based religion accompanied by an emerging priestly class formally began with the Solomon's construction of the Temple. It was approximately 900 B.C.E.

Prior to that time, people, let's call them the descendants of the original tribes who settled in Canaan, what we today call "Israel" several hundred years earlier, had holy objects which they venerated. These objects, the Ark of the Covenant, the staff of Moses, or objects that were worn by the priest and used for divination like the *urim* and *thumim,* were accorded special sanctity. Certain groups of people treasured one object, others another. It was likely, for example, that several holy objects could be housed in the same place but one group would venerate one object and another group, would venerate another. Sacrifices were the normative form of worship and were offered in special local places like Beth El, Shiloh, and Shechem and probably in every town.

Almost immediately following Solomon's death the country split into two. What came to be called Israel, the Northern part, developed or rediscovered its own approach to the biblical religion. Jeroboam its founder, constructed two major temples, one in a place which came to be called Dan and another in Beth El. The Northern Kingdom of Israel lasted until 721 B.C.E. when it was destroyed by the Assyrians. It is likely that some northern priests as well as a number of people migrated south to Jerusalem in order to avoid their imminent destruction. The priests were integrated into

Judean society resulting in the beginning of priestly caste structure which is still present today.

When the Bible is read today a great deal of it focuses on the supremacy of Jerusalem and its criticism of the religion of the Northern Kingdom. This is clearly a polemic. The geography and location of the Northern Kingdom resulted in its being more populated and more prosperous than its southern neighbor (Jerusalem). The Northern Kingdom had significantly larger amounts of arable farm land and was on the international trade routes.

It is somewhat surprising that in spite of the Biblical polemics which decried Northern Israelite religion, that the name "Israel" was chosen for a modern nation state and not "Judah."

Scholars believe that during the First Temple and Babylonian periods that numerous tribes worshipped a God who could have been universal but wasn't exclusive. This was not monotheism (the worship of one god) it was monolatry, a religion that believed in a supreme god that recognized the existence of others. The God of Judah and the God of Israel was understood to be a king, creator, father, warrior and provider of fertilizing rain.

Over time that God, YHVH, acquired a number of names like El and Shaddai that came from some of the surrounding peoples. Scholars believe that YHVH originated in the Amorite region of upper Mesopotamia and could have meant "He who brings into being", in other words "The Creator."

These people worshipped either by praying or by offering sacrifices in local shrines, called high places, or *bamot*. We are not certain if the prayers had words or were tunes which were sung. We believe that First Temple worship took place without a Torah and the concept of Shabbat was still emerging. The oldest form of sacrifice was a whole offering *olah*. There was also a communal offering *shalem,* and a sin offering *hatat*. These offering either occurred in places that communities considered special or in local shrines. This all changed in Babylon.

LEADING UP TO BABYLON:
JOSIAH, JEREMIAH AND EZEKIEL

While it is nearly impossible to pinpoint an exact date when First Temple religion began to morph into what eventually evolved in Babylon into Judaism and became the religion that Ezra brought with him to Jerusalem in 459 B.C.E., a good place to begin would be 164 years earlier in the country of Judah.

It's the year 621 B.C.E. and according to the II Kings and the book of Chronicles, Josiah, a Davidic descendant, was king. The two sources disagree about his age but not about the scroll which was discovered while attempting to cleanse the Temple. On the basis of that newly discovered ancient scroll, Josiah allegedly re-organized his government. He replaced the local system of justice which was ruled by tribal elders with a civil service consisting of priests. He abolished local sacrifices and shrines and insisted that all worship would be conducted in the Temple in Jerusalem and he combined a festival of spring with a festival of unleavened bread into what became the Passover festival.

What was in this scroll that revolutionized Judean society? The scroll was composed of portions of what today is referred to as the book of Deuteronomy. Some of it might have been written earlier and clearly more of it was added on and revised at a later date, but the essence of Josiah's government platform can be found in Deuteronomy 17-29. (For those familiar with the weekly Torah reading, this corresponds to *Shoftim, Ki Tetze,* and *Ki Tavo.*)

Finding or creating a written scroll, which legally outlined how individuals, judges and rulers should behave was a major innovation in the ancient world, and created the basis for what evolved into modern Judaism. These sections of Deuteronomy were the first written parts of what came to be called the Five Books of Moses.

Josiah also capitalized on the dynastic struggles taking place in Assyria and Babylon and successfully reunited Judah and Israel for the first time since its original separation in the tenth century B.C.E. The Bible praises Josiah and considers him to be the man most loved by God since Joshua which makes him more loved even than David. That's hefty praise. Some scholars believe that Josiah's success in the North was because he was aided by the prophet Jeremiah.

The period between 800-400 B.C.E. was a time of extreme change and uncertainty in the Middle East. This change was marked by the rise of a radically new form of political organization, the empire. The first empire in the region was the Assyrians. It was followed by the Neo-Babylonians and then the Persians. These world empires enacted imperial, religious and political policies. They pioneered a procedure which uprooted and resettled entire populations in order to weaken the previous allegiances and loyalties to existing nations.

When Nebuchadnezzar became the emperor of Babylon, what was then referred to as Judah (what we refer to today as "Israel") once again became a satrap, a vassal state. Josiah was actually killed in a battle at Megiddo (Armageddon) defending his Babylonian liege.

The politics of the Middle East rarely changes. Shortly after Josiah's death his successor was approached by the Egyptians who wished to create a buffer between Egypt and Babylon. In exchange for providing military support independence was offered.

Jeremiah preached against it. His views were disregarded and the Persian satrap (Judah) allied with Egypt and rebelled. Nebuchadnezzar wouldn't tolerate rebellion and responded without mercy. He physically uprooted a major portion of the population and transplanted them to a suburb of Babylon called Nippur. It was the year 597 B.C.E. This act is referred to as the Babylonian Exile. Thirteen years later, as a result of Josiah's descendants' additional misbehaving, the Temple was destroyed. It was 586 B.C.E.

This was also the time of the prophet Ezekiel's ministry. Ezekiel was one of the thousands of people exiled to Babylon in 597 B.C.E. From that point onward his prophecies changed from warnings of imminent danger to those offering comfort, consolation and the hope of return.

BABYLONIAN IMPACT

Babylon was the greatest most sophisticated city in the ancient world. It successfully integrated a number of different peoples with different religious beliefs into its culture. This process was a result of their acceptance of the gods and the religious beliefs of conquered peoples into the Babylonian pantheon where Babylonian deities reigned supreme. This system of religious tolerance and integration positioned the current regime as ancient and authentic. The finding of the book of Deuteronomy, where the discovery of an ancient scroll served as the catalyst for governmental reorganization, mirrored the Babylonian model. It also served as a model example for how Judaism successfully adapts over time. Judaism traditionally takes the old and makes it new and takes the new and makes it better.

The developing Judaism didn't just mirror the larger culture; it modified it and repackaged it into a modern framework. For example, the Chief God of the Babylonian pantheon was Marduk, who originally was an Amorite tribal God. As the Babylonian culture developed Marduk gained additional names and stature. His chief accomplishment was that he engaged in a battle against one of the older gods, Tiamat and was victorious. As a result of his victory, Marduk separated her body and created the heavens and the earth.

In Hebrew the equivalent word for Tiamat is *tahom*. It is found in Genesis 1:2. This story was re-enacted and retold in the main Babylonian Temples in Haran and Ur, two places mentioned in the book of Genesis. The Biblical editors transformed that ancient myth into the monotheistic one we have today.

The process of shifting a religion from a polytheistic culture to a monotheistic one, rejecting the belief in many, didn't occur overnight and without compromise. Phrases found in Genesis like, "Let us make man" were fiercely attacked by the prophet referred to as Deutero-Isaiah who understood these phrases as concessions to polytheism. Yet they still remain in our Bible. Similarly, Deuteronomy's statement, the closest to dogma that Judaism has ever adopted, clearly states," Hear O Israel, the Lord our God is alone" a clear push for monotheism over those that claim, "Who is like you among the gods?"

The function and structure of Babylonian religion also paralleled what emerged in Jerusalem as the state religion of the land of Israel. In Babylon, one major god dwelt in a secluded room inside the Temple and was ministered to by a hereditary priesthood. Similarly, in Jerusalem, Temple services were conducted in open courts containing altars and daily, festive, and monthly sacrifices performed by a hereditary priesthood.

The importance of the Babylonian priesthood in the empire influenced the role of the emerging Israelite priesthood and represents one of the two pillars upon which Second Temple and the emerging Bible was positioned.

Babylonian theology similarly influenced Israelite religion. Babylonian theology stressed the importance of goodness, truth, law, justice, freedom, wisdom, learning, courage and loyalty. Mercy and compassion were qualities to be emulated and special protection was accorded to the widows, orphans and strangers, a phrase that is repeated numerous times in the Bible (these values also have parallels in Canaanite theology).

Babylonian theology also understood suffering as being deserved because everyone sinned. In order to improve one's life, expiation came as a result of pleading and confessing to one's personal god. This was not too dissimilar from what we understand to be Second Temple beliefs.

The Israelite religion in the period leading up to the building of the Second Temple clearly was influenced by the exilic experience. The changes which occurred in Judaic Babylon brought to Judea by Ezra included added prohibitions against commerce on Shabbat and prohibitions against intermarriage. To put it simply, Babylon transformed the religion of Judah into Judaism.

WHAT WAS IT THAT OCCURRED IN BABYLON THAT PAVED THE GROUNDWORK FOR JEWISH SURVIVAL?

The most active period of Israelite religious development took place in exile. It was a result of the combination of assimilation into a larger culture and a necessary separation in order to maintain basic beliefs and cultural norms. As a result, for example, Judaism in Babylon adapted and assimilated the names of the Babylonian months, (Nisan, Tishrei, Kislev...) along with Babylonian names, (Esther, Mordecai, Ishtar and Marduk). Similarly Babylonian religious motifs and symbols like cherubim and angels also found their way into biblical texts.

Even while Judaism assimilated and adapted to Babylonian society it also became more insular. People most likely began to engage in communal meals on the Sabbath and possibly refrain from work. It is likely that concepts like the observance of the Sabbath, dietary laws and the study of The Law (Torah) began to develop. Just prior to the ascension of Cyrus, the emperor of Persia and Medea in 539 B.C.E., a newly formulated vision of a return to the land and the Temple's reconstruction began to emerge. It is probable that the Jewish community in exile aided Cyrus's successful overthrow of the previous government, since one of his first acts as Emperor was to grant permission to the Judean exiles and to other peoples to return to their lands and to begin to rebuild their Temples.

It took another eighty years for the constitution (the Torah) to be constructed in a manner that it could be transported by Ezra to Jerusalem and adopted. Second Temple religion was built on the pillars of the Babylonian religious structure and was supported by the Persian state. What emerged in the form of the Torah was a compromise document between the two major ongoing biblical religious traditions, the covenantal religion described in Deuteronomy and the priestly cult.

CONCLUSION

Two different versions explain how Ezra brought the Torah with him from Babylon and they contradict one another. In the Ezra version he arrives in Jerusalem accompanied by priests, prophets and soldiers carrying the Torah. He builds an altar and gathers people from near and far, men women and children. He then proceeds to offer sacrifices according to the Law from morning until evening.

The second version is recorded in the contemporary book of Nehemiah. In that version Ezra returns from Babylon with the Torah. He gathers the people from near and far and builds a platform by the water gate. He is accompanied by priests, Levites and soldiers. The water gate was not on the Temple's premises. The Levites then ascend the platform and teach the word of the Lord from morning until night, to men, women and children, each according to their level of understanding. Following that Ezra proclaims:

This is the day of the Lord rejoice, no longer mourn, eat meat and drink wine for this is the day that the Lord has made.

In the Nehemiah version the prophets are replaced by Levites, the teachers of the Law.

The differences between the Ezra version and the Nehemiah version, priestly sacrificial worship verses the study of the law, the same two tensions that remain with us today, had their origins in Babylonian culture. This was the basic religious tension of Second Temple times.

As the written word, the Torah became a fixture in Jewish religious practice. Scholars and scribes were needed to interpret it. These men came to be
called *sofrim,* scribes. They were the predecessors of what came to be called
rabbis some 400-plus years later.

What is the secret of Judaism's survival? What was it that was gained in Babylon
that has allowed Judaism to continue to adapt to a changing world?

The Jewish people learned to adapt and modify the successes of a majority
culture into a monotheistic framework.

The study of the written word replaced belief in prophets and divination
and provided a basis for faith.

The concept of the Sabbath, a day of rest, a day when time stopped, originated in Babylon and was further developed in Second Temple times.

In summation, the study of sacred texts, the observance of a special day
and the ability to adapt to a constantly changing world brought us to this
moment in time.

THE LAST KINGS OF ISRAEL (JUDAH)

WHAT DOES IT MEAN?

Why has so little emphasis been placed on how the Bible, the source of religious inspiration in the Western world, ends? One would think that it would end upon a motivational and inspirational note that challenges us to pursue peace and perform acts of loving kindness. But it's not the case. The Bible's (what Christians call the Old Testament) final books, are the two books of Chronicles. The final acts in these books focus on the end of the Davidic line in Babylon in the period just after the Temple's destruction.

A few books in the Bible allegedly postdate these events: Haggai, Zechariah, Malachi, Daniel, Esther, Ezra and Nehemiah. Haggai, Zechariah and Malachi were the last of the prophets and their ministries focused on the circumstances leading up to and immediately following the rebuilding of the Second Temple. They are linked with the books of Ezra and Nehemiah. The books of Daniel and Esther focus on life during the Babylonian captivity, even though they were composed hundreds of years later.

Chronicles is the final book in the Canon and it is paralleled by 1 and 2 Kings. Both works are, or at least appear to be, religious histories leading up to the Temple's destruction and its immediate aftermath. Both books conclude with the story of Gedaliah, the last governor of Judah, a person who was not of Davidic lineage, followed by a series of appendices that explain what happened to the last of David's line, the children of the late King Josiah.

Three appendixes are attached to the end of the II Chronicles. The third and final one ends on a note of hope. It announces the ascendancy of Cyrus as king of Babylon who authorizes the return to Israel and the rebuilding of the Temple. Chronicles understood the return from exile as a fulfillment of God's promise to the patriarchs.

The Bible ends with an unanswered question. Wasn't the Messiah was supposed to be one of David's descendants and if that's the case shouldn't he or his progeny still be around? Jewish tradition doesn't have an easy answer. Christianity does.

There are legends that claim some of the famous Jewish historical personalities were David's descendants but if that were the case shouldn't more people know about it? Or is it a big, big secret, like the Knights Templar would have kept?

There is one example in the Bible of legendary descendants being involved in an ongoing historical Frodo-like struggle, and that's the story of Purim. Jewish liturgy connects the struggle between Moses and Amalek with the battle between Saul, the first King of Israel and Agag, King of the Amalekites a span of approximately two hundred years. This mythological struggle is continued by Agag's descendent, Haman the Agagite who battles Mordecai the son of Kish a metaphorical descendant of King Saul the son of Kish. Of course this battle took place in Persia many hundreds of years later and in a country nearly one thousand miles away. This is great mythology; not history.

The books of 2 Kings and 2 Chronicles describe the end of David's line taking place in Babylon in a manner that leaves us asking basic questions: What is the reason the Bible chronicles nearly six hundred years of Davidic kingship and then allows it to end in an insignificant if not pathetic way? What is the reason for this unsatisfying ending to the story? Can there be a lesson that we have missed?

What follows is a brief summary of the final chapters of Chronicles and Kings. Following that, I will offer some concluding remarks. Hopefully this will clarify some of those issues.

The last great king of Israel was Josiah. He peacefully united the north and the south and restructured the government. He was killed in a battle with

Egyptians while fighting on behalf of his liege lord, Nebuchadnezzar, King of Babylon. Josiah was succeeded by his son Jehoahaz and it appears that Judah's sovereignty was transferred from Babylon to Egypt.

As soon as Jehoahaz became king, Pharaoh Neco imprisoned him and moved him to Egypt where he remained a prisoner until he died. Clearly, Jehoahaz was a threat to Egyptian expansion and as a consequence never had the opportunity to rule from Jerusalem. Pharaoh Neco appointed another of Josiah's sons to rule in his stead. His name was Eliakim, Neco changed his name to Jehoikim and forced him to pay a per capita tax to Egypt. Jehoikim reigned in Jerusalem for eleven years. In the last three years of his reign the world changed and Judah once again became a Babylonian possession. It is the year 605 B.C.E.

Approximately three years later, Nebuchadnezzar was forced to return to Babylon to deal with local affairs and Jehoikim, most likely with promised support from Egypt, rebelled. At this point the texts are unclear but we are told that Jehoikim died peacefully and was succeeded by his son, Jehoiachin.

Nebuchadnezzar advanced on Jerusalem to put down the rebellion and Jehoiachin wisely surrendered thus saving Jerusalem from destruction. It was 597 B.C.E. Along with thousands of people, he was taken into exile and Judah (Jerusalem) needed a ruler.

Nebuchadnezzar appointed another of Josiah's sons, Mattaniah to serve as king and in accordance with the customs of the time, changed his name to Zedekiah. Zedekiah reigned from 597-586 BCE.

Zedekiah, perhaps seeking independence (though one wonders why), joined an alliance with the Phoenicians and the leaders of the coastal countries, and along with them planned a revolt. Nebuchadnezzar reacted swiftly and marched on Judah it was 589-587 B.C.E.

Nebuchadnezzar besieged Jerusalem and built towers around the city. The siege lasted seventeen months during which famine took root. The walls of the north side of the city were breached on the ninth day of the month of Tammuz. Years later the rabbis established the Fast of seventeenth of Tammuz, explaining that the Babylonians entered the city eight days after the walls had been breached.

Zedekiah and his household fled the city. They were apprehended near Jericho and placed on trial. His sons were slaughtered in front of him and following that his eyes were removed. He was placed in chains and brought to Babylon.

The siege of Jerusalem continued into the next month, and on the seventh day of the month of Av, access was gained to the Temple. It was set aflame on the eve of the ninth of Av and it burned through the tenth. Nebuchadnezzar appointed Gedaliah, son of Ahikam, to be in charge of those who remained. Gedaliah was not of Davidic (Josianic) descent. As governor he established a government at Mitzpah but was slaughtered by a pro-Davidic faction who resented being ruled by a non-Davidic leader.

As a result of his death, the rabbis established a fast in his name which takes place immediately following the New Year Festival, the fast of Gedaliah.

Both Chronicles and Kings end by explaining that Jehoiachin, Josiah's remaining descendant who had been in exile since 597 B.C.E., was eventually raised to a new status. He was provided with new clothes, more regular food and according to one source, permitted to dine at the king's table. This has been interpreted by some to indicate that a minor sort of reconciliation occurred in Babylon and that a source of hope remained for the Jewish people.

But the story doesn't end here. One final descendant of David was still alive. His name was Zerubbabel, a descendant of Jehoiachin, the one who surrendered to Nebuchadnezzar. Zerubbabel, according to the book of the prophet Zechariah, participated in the Temple's rebuilding. This allows us to date him living sometime after 539 B.C.E. and prior to 516 B.C.E. when the Temple was completed.

He is mentioned in the *haftarah* that is read on Hanukkah that follows the description of the candelabra fashioned by the Levites in book of Numbers. The Persian Empire was in disarray. King Darius faced rebellion in Media, Babylonia, Egypt and Asia Minor. Perhaps the prophets of the time thought that God was once again intervening in history as they thought when Cyrus became emperor and authorized the Temple's rebuilding. Perhaps they thought that the long awaited Davidic restoration was about to occur.

Zerubbabel, had been officially appointed governor of Yehud (Judah). The prophet Haggai explicitly identifies him as the long expected Davidic savior who would usher in a new era. The prophet Zechariah links him with the successful completion of the Temple, and refers to him as the "righteous branch."

> *Behold, the man whose name is the Branch: for he shall grow up in his place and he shall build the Temple of the Lord. He shall sit on the throne and a priest shall be by his throne, and a peaceful understanding shall be between them.* (Zechariah 6:12-13).

The vision of a people being ruled by a king had been altered in Babylon. Zechariah envisions the leadership of restored Jerusalem being shared by king and priest. A compromise had been reached between secular and religious authority. The Temple was completed and restored in 516 B.C.E. and so too does Zerubbabel.

It is unclear why he disappears. It could have been because those in power somewhere didn't wish the threat of a rebellion to occur. What is clear is that by the end of the sixth century B.C.E. the house of David came to an end.

The appendix added in Chronicles which mentions Cyrus and his permitting the return to Jerusalem and the rebuilding of the Temple in 539 B.C.E. was an additional sign of hope. But the Davidic line, the line from which the Messiah would come, had for all intent vanished. Never again would Israel/Judah have a King.

And that means if the Messianic time is to occur it would most be likely be a result of an attitudinal shift. That's right, the Messiah could not be a person because the Davidic line has vanished.

Perhaps that's the lesson that can be learned from the story of the last kings of Judah. That change, will only occur as a result of the way people behave.

AND WHY THIS STORY ISN'T GOOD FOR...

As of this writing, only two Samaritan communities, one in the city of Holon just outside of Tel Aviv and the other on Mount Gerizim, are all that remain of the people once called Samaritans. Their numbers at last count were just fewer than eight hundred. The challenge of their continuity has never been greater. All of its constituents are descended from four families and as a result genetic disease is extremely common. Samaritans refuse to accept converts and only recently (in an effort to increase their gene pool) have agreed to permit men from Samaritan families to marry woman outside of the fold. These people are usually Israeli women and they will be accepted only if they agree to follow Samaritan religious practices.

Women who wish to align themselves with the Samaritan community undergo a six month trial period before officially being accepted. It isn't easy since the Samaritan interpretation of biblical (Levitical) laws is more stringent than those practiced in the Haredi communities. They actually must live separately in separate houses during their menstrual period and after childbirth. A small number of Ukrainian woman have recently been allowed to marry into this community in an additional effort to expand the gene pool.

The community is governed by a high priest who is selected by from the priestly family that lives on Mount Gerizim, the same mountain that, according to the Bible, Moses ordering Joshua to take the Twelve Tribes of Israel to the mountains by Nablus and place half of the tribes on the top of Mount Gerizim, the Mount of Blessing, and the other half in Mount Ebal, the Mount of the Curse. This story is found in Deuteronomy 11:29 and 27:12.

The likelihood of the future of the Samaritan community is bleak but who are/were they? What influence did they have on the development of Judaism? Why are so many Christians familiar with the parable of The Good Samaritan and why are so many Jews not?

WHO ARE THE SAMARITANS?

Two possible origins of the term Samaritan exist. The word shomron means guardian and the Samaritans consider themselves to be the guardians of The Law. The early Christian Fathers (Eusibius, Jerome and Origin) agree they took this name in order to protect The Law from the interpretations of the Talmudic rabbis. Others claim that the name Samaritan was derived as a result of the naming of the recently conquered Northern Israel (Samaria) by the Assyrians in 722 B.C.E.

The Samaritans claim to be the Israelite descendants of the Northern tribes of Ephraim and Manasseh. This possibly could be true because the Assyrians only deported and resettled selected populations of the lands they conquered and recent genetic testing authenticates their ancient status.

Samaritan history claims the separation or the schism which divided them from the Israelites occurred after Joshua's death when Eli, the priest left the tabernacle which Moses had constructed on Mount Gerizim and build another one in the hills of Shiloh. The Samaritans retained the original Ark and separated themselves from their/our cousins. They consider themselves direct descendants of the Joseph tribes (Ephraim and Menasseh) and claim to be directly descended from Aaron, through Eleazar and Pinchas. They claim to be the true Israel descendants of the Ten Lost tribes' and believe that their version of the Bible is the original that was falsified by the Jewish people during the Babylonian exile. This, of course, is subject to dispute.

Historically the Samaritans emerged as a religious and ethnic community sometime after the Assyrian conquest even though some date their split to the time of Nehemiah and Ezra and the building of the Second Temple after the Babylonian exile.

It is interesting to note that both Jewish and Samaritans religious leaders taught it was wrong to have contact with one another and neither should speak to one another or enter their respective territories. Josephus sights numerous violent confrontations between both groups through the first half of the first century C.E. Under the Roman Empire Samaria was part of the Roman ruled province of Judaea. They appear briefly in the Christian gospels in the form of the parable of The Good Samaritan.

SAMARITAN BELIEFS

The Samaritans have a Torah which they claim is the only inspired text. Their literature also consists of historical writings and books containing legal codes and legendary texts which we refer to as midrash. They had a Temple on Mount Gerizim that was destroyed in 128 B.C.E. by John Hyrcanus. It existed for about 200 years and was later rebuilt after the Bar Kokba revolt around 135 C.E. It is now mostly believed that the Samaritan Temple was actually constructed in the Persian period, probably as early as the first half of the fifth century B.C.E. and that it was devoted to the God of Israel and perhaps, not surprisingly, was strikingly similar to the descriptions of the Temple in Jerusalem.

The Samaritans believe in one God, YHWH, who gave the Torah to Moses on Mount Gerizim. They also believe that resurrection will occur at the End of Days and the loyal will go to Paradise. Their priests are the interpreters of The Law, the keeper of traditions, and they accept only their versions of the five books of Moses as holy texts. They have a different version of the Ten Commandments (e.g. their tenth commandments is about the sanctity of Mount Gerizim). They retain ancient Hebrew script, eat lamb at Passover and celebrate Aviv as the spring and *Yom Teruah* at the beginning of Tishrei. They refer to themselves as *B'nai Israel* but not *Yehudim*.

From the time of Ezra and Nehemiah (the Persian period), we learn of continual Samaritan hostility toward the rebuilding of the Jerusalem and the establishment of the Temple. After all, the inhabitants of Samaria considered themselves to be members of the tribes of Ephraim and Manasseh who were not deported by the Assyrians while the Jerusalem priesthood understood them to be pagan descendants of the foreign peoples who had been brought in and resettled in this area by Assyrian kings.

The Samaritan influence, while hostile to the Jewish people, remained minimal until the codification of Christian scripture in which the parable of the Good Samaritan was inserted into the tenth chapter of the book of Luke and served as one of many catalysts for anti-Jewish behavior.

The parable followed what is referred to as "the great commandment" which sets the stage for the derogatory description that follows:

Behold, a certain teacher of the law stood up and tested him, saying, Teacher, what shall I do to inherit eternal life?
He said to him, What is written in the law? How do you read it?
He answered, You shall love the Lord your God with all your heart, with all your soul, with all your strength, with all your mind, [Deuteronomy 6:5]; and your neighbor as yourself [Leviticus 19:18].
He said to him, You have answered correctly. Do this, and you will live.
But he, desiring to justify himself, asked Jesus, Who is my neighbor?"
(Luke 10:25–29)

Jesus replied with this parable:

A certain man was going down from Jerusalem to Jericho, and he fell among robbers, who both stripped him and beat him, and departed, leaving him half dead. By chance a certain priest was going down that way. When he saw him, he passed by on the other side. In the same way a Levite also, when he came to the place, and saw him, passed by on the other side. But a certain Samaritan, as he travelled, came where he was. When he saw him, he was moved with compassion, came to him, and bound up his wounds, pouring on oil and wine. He set him on his own animal, and brought him to an inn, and took care of him. On the next day, when he departed, he took out two denari, and gave them to the host, and said to him, "Take care of him. Whatever you spend beyond that, I will repay you when I return."

Now which of these three do you think seemed to be a neighbor to him who fell among the robbers?

He said, He who showed mercy on him.
Then Jesus said to him, Go and do likewise.

This parable ostensibly taught by Jesus, tells the story of a person, an expert in The Law, who is tested by Jesus. The expert in The Law is a euphemism for a rabbinic scholar. Jesus tells him the story of a man who was robbed and beaten and then left on the road. He indicates that first a priest (a Cohen), and then a Levite pass him by and refuse to offer to help and aid him. The third person to encounter him on the road was a Samaritan who promptly comes to his assistance. The parable portrays the rabbinic scholar as a novice and then derides both the Cohen and the Levite for in appropriate behavior. This simple parable was one of many examples found in Christian scripture that reinforced Christian practice at the expense of the Jewish community.

The Samaritans are our cousins, a distant offshoot of what came to be known as the Jewish people. They followed a more stringent interpretation of The Law, much like the Sadducees and the Karaites who followed centuries later. In each instance, with each of these peoples, a strict nearly literal interpretation of The Law resulted in their playing a diminishing role in history. The Pharisees are the political party which served as the counterpart or opposition to the Sadducees. Their name was derived from the Hebrew word perush, which means having the ability to interpret. The spiritual descendants of the Pharisees were what today we call rabbis. It was the ability to interpret The Law, to recognize that The Law was constantly evolving to meet the needs of changing times which is one of the reasons we are here today.

HOW THE RABBIS WON

It seems that I must have missed a major class when I was in Rabbinical School because until recently I didn't have a clue how Jewish life existed and functioned after the destruction of the Second Temple. As a student of Jewish history and one who has always believed that lessons could be learned through the study of Jewish history, my inability to understand and extrapolate theories following the destruction of the Second Temple to the modern period left me at a loss to conjecture how and why Judaism continued to develop.

How was it that after the destruction of the Second Temple in Roman times, an act which left the Jewish community without any central authority, any governing body, that the rabbis emerged as the guiding force?

We know that Johanan ben Zakkai's academy in Yavneh did not receive one hundred percent support from the established community. We also know that following the Temple's destruction that Johanan's academy wasn't the only attempt to insure Jewish continuity. The ruling powers in Jerusalem certainly didn't support his efforts; after all, they chose to remain in the city, while he secretly escaped in a coffin. This causes me to ask "why did the academy strategy succeed when others failed?" Why was the academy strategy victorious and perhaps most importantly, were there any lessons, any items of import which can be gleaned from that experience?

In order to understand this, it is necessary to have a sense of the way the Middle East was divided in the Roman period. Prior to Rome's ascendancy the ancient world was ruled by Greece. When Alexander the Great died without heir, his generals divided his empire into four kingdoms. One of his generals was named Ptolemy, he established the Ptolemied dynasty in Egypt. Another was Seleucid who inherited or claimed Persia. By the second century Rome had established a center in Constantinople which bordered on the Parthian empire. The Parthians (Babylon) were the successors to the Seulicids. Relations between these two empires were rarely peaceful. When the Second Temple was destroyed by the Romans and in the aftermath of the Bar Kokba rebellion, a major population shift occurred from Palestine to Babylon.

Jewish life beginning with the exile in 597 B.C.E and followed by the destruction of the first Temple thirteen years later, thrived in Babylon, the Torah was compiled and our people were permitted to return to Palestine and rebuild the Temple primarily because the Babylonian rulers desired it. It was logical for the Jewish population, when fleeing the Romans, to return to Babylon.

The Parthians, the successor to the Babylonians and the Medians encouraged travel to Palestine ostensibly to provide the leadership of the Jewish community with the opportunity to receive instruction in a new form of learning. This form of learning was called the Mishnah. In the beginning of the third century C.E. Rabbi Judah HaNasi in Galilee completed the process of editing the Mishnah, a process which had been ongoing during the preceding three centuries in Roman Palestine. This effort paralleled the development of Roman law. The Mishnah was supplemented by the Mishnah of Avot, often called the Ethics of the Fathers, where in its first chapter it provides a detailed description of how authority was transmitted. From Moses to Joshua, to the elders, Prophets, to the men of the Great Assembly and into Mishnaic times thus demonstrating the continuity of David's descendants. With the creation of the Mishnah the rabbis succeeded in establishing their authority or at least their presence as a major factor in the Jewish world.

Jews played an important role in mid-first century Middle Eastern politics, not only in Palestine but in Armenia and specifically Babylonia. Jewish support was important for those ruling in Babylonia, the Parthians, both for empire stability and in the area of foreign affairs. Parthia, the successor to Media, bordered and was often in conflict with Rome. Rome controlled Palestine and supported the creation of the academy at Yavneh. It was theoretically important for the Parthians to encourage Jews to travel to Palestine to receive instruction for a variety of political reasons including that the Jewish population in Palestine was not supportive of Roman policies leading up to and following the Bar Kohkba rebellion. The reference in the *Haggadah* of the clandestine meeting in Bnei Brak reflects the anti-Roman activity leading up to the revolt.

Practically it provided the Parthian leadership with important information about the Roman Empire with whom they were fighting on their western borders.

Babylon and Jerusalem, Palestine and Babylonia, two different cultures, two different centers, two different versions of the Talmud, each guided by different theologies and different political establishments. One governed by the Romans, the other by whoever ruled in Babylonia.

In addition to being linked by common ancestry these two populations were also linked through the Bible. The Bible as we understand it is based upon two pillars. The first is the importance of the priestly role. The second is the importance of the Davidic genetic line. Davidic lineage was a prerequisite for ruling and even though it was violated from time to time, each ruler, whether high priest or Exilarch was required somehow to be connected to David. This is evinced at the end of the second book of Kings and in the book of Chronicles where, in spite of the exile and destruction, we are informed that the Davidic bloodline continues.

In the thirty-seventh year of the exile of King Jehoichin of Judah, King Evil-merodach of Babylon, took note of King Jehoichin and released him from prison. He spoke kindly to him, and gave him a throne above those of other kings who were with him in Babylon. His prison garments were removed, and he received regular rations by his favor for the rest of his life. (2 Kings 25:27)

The descendants of Jehoichin: the captive and his son...... (Chronicles 3:17)

THE RELATIONSHIP BETWEEN THE PATRIARCHATE AND THE EXILARCHATE

The Babylonian Talmud developed between the third and seventh centuries and reflected the Parthian, Sassanid and eventually Arab cultures that rule Mesopotamia; while the Jerusalem Talmud more closely resembled Roman

culture. It stands to reason that the Romans nurtured and supported rabbinic culture which was led by a Patriarch, while the Parthians followed a
Babylonian model and created an institution called, "the Exilarch." The
Exilarchate in Parthian Babylon, like the Patriarchate in Roman Palestine,
was the most convenient means for both Rome and Babylon to manage a
potentially useful ethnic group's affairs at home and abroad. Following the
defeat of the rebellion a huge population shift occurred and those surviving the rebellion left Palestine and migrated to Babylonia. It is 135 C.E. and the
Babylonian community is beginning to emerge as the major center of Jewish life.

Less than one hundred years later Rav, who was Babylonian born, returned
from studying in Palestine and established an academy in Sura in 219.C.E.
in order to teach the Mishnaic system. His younger counterpart, Samuel, worked with the ruling authorities in Babylon and created the famous
phrase, "the law of the land is the law" thus formalizing the relationship
between the Jewish community and the ruling government. Samuel must
have been acting on behalf of Romans supported the rabbinic culture which
it had nurtured while the Parthians and those that followed, supported a
more organized centrally governed structure that paralleled their society.

THE ORIGINS OF THE EXILARCH

The Exilarch (also referred to as the Resh Galuta) was the leading authority
of the Jewish community in Babylonia. The origins of this office are ob-
scure and we lack any sources from the time of the destruction of the First
Temple (586 B.C.E.) to the destruction of the Second Temple (70 C.E.) It
has been established that the title Exilarch was held at least until 1258 C.E.
when the Mongols sacked Baghdad. The major sources referring to the
Exilarch are found in the Babylonian Talmud through the sixth century,
Palestinian sources through the ninth century, and Pahlavi documents. The
Pahlavi, or Parthians, were a dynasty that captured Iran and Iraq from the
Romans in the third century B.C.E. They took over the bureaucracy of the
Selucids, Greek rulers who succeeded Alexander. Other sources referring to
the Exilarch are found in Seder Olam Zuta and works of Rav Sherira Gaon
and the Cairo Geniza.

There are a number of theories regarding the creation of this position.
Professor Jacob Neusner dates it around 79 C.E. He suggests that the position was created by a Parthian king named Vologases who, following the

destruction of the Second Temple created the position as a way to govern the Jewish community. This could be the case because after the Second Temple was destroyed large numbers of people fled Judah and migrated to Babylon.

Evidence exists that Hananiah the nephew of Joshua b. Hananiah intercalated the calendar in 145 C.E. This could have been authorized by a leader of the community, possibly, an Exilarch. The first actual reference in the Talmud to the *Resh Galuta* refers to Rav Huna as the Exilarch. This was in the third century corresponding to the time of Judah Ha Nasi. Judah Ha Nasi, who claimed Davidic descent through the female line, said, "if Huna came to Palestine he would give him precedence for Huna descended from male line of David". Neusner and others assume that it was reasonable that the Exilarch existed during the last one hundred fifty years of Parthian rule. Each group claimed Davidic descent. This did not appear to be a recipe designed for success.

The Parthians were succeeded by the Sassanid's and the Exilarchate was structured in a way that reflected Sassanid society. The Exilarch had executive powers but no real authority. Subject to the whims of the ruling powers he served as the voice of the Jewish people (that is when the rabbis weren't interfering). He was able to enforce decisions of rabbinical courts, appoint judges and at times able to authorize corporal punishment. He was able to attempt to regulate economic life, appoint overseers in the market place and was able to give rabbis privileged places in market place to sell their produce.

The differences in cultures between the rabbinate, (eventually the Gaonite), and the Exilarch began possibly as a partnership to justify the authenticity of both groups to the normal Jew and, according to Neusner, to overcome the authority and influence of the wealthy aristocratic Jews that had achieved prominence in the Parthian empire. The Exilarch presented itself as the representative of the ancient tradition of Moses. When people heard his words they were obeying the Torah of Moses. In order to strengthen this claim, he enlisted the learned, charismatic Palestinian rabbis, also descendants of David. By the end of the third century, the Exilarch provided the chief source of financial support for academies and employment for their graduates.

Stemming from two different cultures each group's theology was based upon different world views. The Exilarch, a Davidic descendent and the political leader of the Jews, believed the Exilarchate would be the instrument through which the restoration of the Jewish people, the Messiah, would occur. This happening would come at an appropriate time and through his line.

The rabbis, many of whom also claimed Davidic descent, believed that along with the written Torah revealed to Moses that an oral unwritten Torah had been preserved and transmitted from prophets to sages and finally to the rabbis, who were the only ones who could understand God's will. Their claim rested on upon their belief in the Oral Torah. Both parties claimed authority. One could say that the rabbis sought to reform the life of Israel so it would conform with the Torah as they taught it. They believed that if Israel lived according to the will of God, History would come to an end and peace and prosperity would result. The matter came to a head in the third century when the rabbis claimed exemption as priests from paying taxes. Eventually, due to the threat that the government might act punitively they capitulated to the Exilarch.

When the Sassanid's succeeded the Parthians, the spiritual function of rabbis and the communal functions of the Exilarch became less well defined and even less so during the period of Arab rule. A clear description of the functions and authority of the Exilarchate under Arab rule has yet to be found. A critical turning point occurred after Karaite schism in 825 C.E. when ruling authorities permitted small religious groups autonomy. From that time onward the Exilarchs were challenged by the Geonim.

WHY DID THE RABBIS WIN?

Why did Vespasian agree and permit Yohanan ben Zakkai to establish an academy in Yavneh? Because he was familiar with the model. Roman culture had adopted and integrated the academy concept from their predecessors the Greeks. As Rome expanded into Europe and imposed its Greco-Roman culture upon Europe, Roman seats of learning spread. These events were paralleled by the Jewish community and academies, places of learning, spread through-out Europe. Overtime they came to be called yeshivas or Seminaries while the Exilarchate which was tied to a ruling more eastern governing structure eventually dissembled and disappeared. That's how the rabbinate and rabbinic authority came to be.

LESSONS

It's interesting. When one studies Talmud the question rarely arises if the rabbis had any real power. Did the rabbis have any ability at any time to shape the course of nations? They did not. From the Second Temple's destruction until the modern era the rabbis and the Jewish people were a powerless microcosm operating under its own rules and always subject to a ruling power. At the same time in each instance, our thinking and our behaviors were impacted by the majority culture.

If there is a lesson to be learned perhaps it is that the different world views of the rabbis and the Exilarch reflects two different ways of understanding what is happening to Jewish life today. The Exilarchic way suggests we should continue as we have. The existing institutions have and will continue to be successful. The Rabbinic view, attempted to change the world. It ran counter to the prevailing view of the majority culture and preached that we should live a life in the manner that they envisioned.

I seriously doubt that existing and future generations can prosper by upholding what has been in hopes it will continue. On the other hand, it is possible that a new vision of how Jews and the institutions that support them/us could be envisioned along with the appropriate language, skill sets and tools. Perhaps multiple views and visions are necessary to attract, integrate, and acculturate the many forms and identities of being Jewish that have come into existence in the past fifty years. One that acknowledges and respects those who emerged from the Former Soviet Union, from Africa, from the European descendants of the Holocaust, and from the rapidly changing dynamic of what we once understood as families.

ENDNOTE

What began with the construction of the Ark of the Covenant brought us to Mitzpah where the judge, prophet, priest and kingmaker Samuel was approached and the people demanded that he appoint a king. It concluded in Shiloh with the death of Gedaliah or perhaps in Babylon with Zerubbabel. With it the history of Judea and the Israelite kings came to an end.

When Ezra and Nehemiah left Babylon to re-establish religious and national life in Judah, what they really brought with them, in addition to the Torah, was Babylonian Judaism.

Babylon, Babylon, Babylon, it all comes back to Babylon. But what lessons are there for us to learn? What is the point of all the stories with which we have been raised (but that they didn't necessarily teach us in Hebrew school)?

Each of the incidents and stories shared in this work suggest lessons that can be learned. When we study the stories of the last kings of Israel we witness the repetition of petty kings with heads full of petty thoughts. Were they motivated by delusions of grandeur? Did they really think that a conquered city could be re-established and its people could live in peace and prosperity? Did they even consider the lessons of their own history? Shouldn't they have learned from the past and perhaps conceived of the world in broader terms?

The last kings of Judah continuously demonstrated weak ineffective leadership. They certainly didn't remember the success of their ancestor Manasseh who ruled a country peacefully for more than fifty years. Nor did they recall the vision, planning and leadership that Josiah and Hezekiah inspired.

The personalities in the Bible are often viewed as leadership paradigms but they rarely are looked at closely or in context. There is a context in which to view the biblical personalities, the ones whose stories are told in the books of Judges, Samuel and Kings.

King Saul, King David, and King Solomon each demonstrate the needs, strengths and weaknesses of people thrust into leadership positions. Saul was positioned in a manner that he could never be successful. David's initial vision or the vision that created him was overpowered by his personal needs and desires. Solomon learned much from his father but failed, like his father, to educate his successor and in doing so damaged his kingdom. Much of the books of Samuel and Kings focus on incidents around which leaders or would-be leaders need to make decisions. How well this was accomplished isn't our concern, but the lessons that can be learned from their stories provide us with much to consider.

Ezra and Nehemiah brought us out of Babylon into what would become a new phase of Jewish life. Their stories suggest not only different leadership models but different visions of how a people should worship.

As our holy text came to be compiled, its authors wove together facts and stories and created myths which would successfully bring together a disparate people and unite them in place, mission, and faith, a faith which would guide their descendants, the rabbis, into different worlds as the future continued to unfold.

The process of unraveling our texts and bringing the knowledge that our historians and archeologists bring to light reveals one of our people's great tools and catalysts for spiritual connection.

For those of us who continue to question, to doubt, I would hope that the reading of this work helped you to engage, connect and better understand the values which we hold so dear.

CHARLES SIMON
September 2016

FJMC PUBLICATIONS

FJMC's publications are available through its website store at www.fjmc.org. Books marked with an asterisk * are available in electronic form through links on the FJMC site.

Biblical Leadership After Moses: Lessons to be Learned*
By Rabbi Charles Simon

"This wonderful collection of essays offers principles of effective leadership for volunteers in any organization. ... these principles of leadership are clearly and persuasively detailed in a highly readable and accessible format."

> DR. RON WOLFSON, Fingerhut Professor of Education, American Jewish University; and author, *Relational Judaism: Using the Power of Relationships to Transform the Jewish Community*

Understanding the Haftarot: An Every person's Guide*
By Rabbi Charles Simon

"If the Haftarot are to reclaim their rightful place as a primary pedagogic tool for uncovering and imagining the Torah's deep truths for the modern synagogue attendee, then Rabbi Simon's exquisite, erudite and thorough introduction to the material offers an essential backdrop to each of us, clergy and layperson alike."

> AARON ALEXANDER, Dean Ziegler School of Rabbinic Studies American Jewish University

Keruv Initiative Series

Engaging The Non-Jewish Spouse: Strategies for Clergy and Lay Leadership provides a step-by-step guide to inclusion taking into consideration the unique culture of each community. It suggests questions that should be discussed by a synagogue's leadership and serves as tool to further engage and guide a Board of Directors.

Intermarriage: Concepts and Strategies for Families and Synagogue Leaders*

Does Keruv have an ideology and theology? And if so what is it? This is themost current thinking about intermarriage to date, an important read for family members and community leaders who wish to effectively work with intermarrieds or potential intermarrieds.

Hearing Men's Voices

Jewish Men at the Crossroads* addresses the many issues facing modern Jewish men, intermarriage, co-parenting, sexual dysfunction, retirement, and the evolving role of men.

"This volume boldly asks the questions in public that the community is privately wondering about Jewish men, their family roles and their future place in the synagogue and Jewish community."

RABBI KERRY OLITZKY, Executive Director of the Jewish Outreach Institute and author

Hearing Men's Voices books contain essays and programs designed to stimulate discussions and involvement in structured program activities directly related to the issues confronting Jewish men. The books are:

Work and Worth

Body and Spirit

Our Fathers/Ourselves

Listening to God's Voice

Leadership - Innovation - Community

The **Federation of Jewish Men's Clubs'** (FJMC) mission is to involve Jewish Men in Jewish Life by building and strengthening Men's Clubs in the Conservative/Masorti Movement. We accomplish this mission by:

Leadership: mentoring leaders at the club, region and international level,

Innovation: developing programming that better connects people of all ages to the Jewish community,

Community: forming meaningful long-lasting relationships based on camaraderie, common interests and core values.

The **FJMC** empowers its members, Jewish men and their families, to become more passionately engaged in Conservative/Masorti Jewish life. Its programmatic initiatives transform individuals and synagogues into more vibrant communities across the globe.

Website: www.fjmc.org
Facebook: FJMC_HQ
Twitter: @FJMC_HQ
LinkedIn: http://www.linkedin.com/company/fjmc

Copyright © 2016 Federation of Jewish Men's Clubs, Inc.
Federation of Jewish Men's Clubs
475 Riverside Drive, Suite 832 New York, NY 10115

ISBN
978-0-935665-13-0 – Paperback
978-0-935665-14-7 – E-book

Made in the USA
Middletown, DE
22 June 2021